Submit Now

Designing Persuasive Web Sites

Contents at a Glance

D1507232

Submit Now

Designing Persuasive Web Sites

Andrew Chak

201 West 103rd Street, Indianapolis, Indiana 46290
An Imprint of Pearson Education
Boston • Indianapolis • London • Munich • New York • San Francisco

Submit Now: Designing Persuasive Web Sites

Copyright © 2003 by New Riders Publishing

International Standard Book Number: 0-7357-1170-4

Library of Congress Catalog Card Number: 200109118

Printed in the United States of America

First edition: September 2002

06 05 04 03 02   7 6 5 4 3 2 1

Interpretation of the printing code: The rightmost double-digit number is the year of the book's printing; the rightmost single-digit number is the number of the book's printing. For example, the printing code 02-1 shows that the first printing of the book occurred in 2002.

Trademarks

Warning and Disclaimer

PUBLISHER
David Dwyer

ASSOCIATE PUBLISHER
Stephanie Wall

EDITOR IN CHIEF
Chris Nelson

EXECUTIVE EDITOR
Steve Weiss

PRODUCTION MANAGER
Gina Kanouse

MANAGING EDITOR
Sarah Kearns

ACQUISITIONS EDITOR
Michael J. Nolan

PRODUCT MARKETING MANAGER
Tammy Detrich

PUBLICITY MANAGER
Susan Nixon

DEVELOPMENT EDITOR
Kathy Murray

COPY EDITOR
Amy Lepore

SENIOR INDEXER
Cheryl Lenser

PROOFREADER
Ben Lawson

COMPOSITION
Kim Scott

MANUFACTURING COORDINATOR
Jim Conway

INTERIOR DESIGNER
Kim Scott

COVER DESIGNER
Aren Howell

MEDIA DEVELOPER
Jay Payne

*To God, who has given me more than I've ever deserved
and makes all things possible.*

*To my parents, for teaching me to work hard to make
the possibilities a reality.*

*To my wife, Eng, for her constant love and devotion that
makes all the possibilities worth pursuing.*

Table of Contents

About the Author

Andrew Chak is a user-experience design consultant and has designed web sites for American Express, IBM, General Motors, Fleet Bank, and Metavante. He is a frequent speaker at web usability and design conferences and has lectured throughout North America. His multidisciplinary background as a graphic interface designer and an industrial engineer gives him a holistic perspective on site design and makes it very difficult for him to explain to others exactly what he does for a living.

About the Technical Reviewer

Carolyn Snyder has 18 years of experience in the software industry and has spent the past eight years practicing user-centered methods, especially usability testing and paper prototyping. In March 1999, Carolyn started Snyder Consulting < www.snyderconsulting.net > to specialize in hands-on work with software and web site development teams. In 2000, Carolyn collaborated with Jakob Nielsen on an e-commerce usability study of twenty b2c (business-to-consumer) sites and co-authored the book *E-commerce User Experience*.

Prior to becoming a usability professional, Carolyn spent 10 years working as a software engineer and project manager at Landis & Staefa, a building controls company. Carolyn has a B.S. in computer science from the University of Illinois and an M.B.A. from the University of Chicago.

Acknowledgments

This book would not have been possible without the help and support (and, in some cases, patience) of quite a few people. Special thanks go to:

- Michael Nolan for persuading me to write this book in the first place (and he didn't even have to resort to any of the tips in this book).

- Kathy Murray, my development editor, for being a constant source of helpful suggestions and encouragement.

- Carolyn Snyder, my technical editor, for not pulling any punches (or nits) to make this a better book.

- Victoria Elzey, Sarah Kearns, and the team at New Riders for keeping me on schedule (or at least trying to) and off the streets.

- Heidi Adkisson, Don Braithwaite, Don Hameluck, Easby Ho, Michael Kim, and William Munroe for providing honest and thought-provoking feedback as my advance readers.

- My coworkers in UXD who always make my workday interesting.

- My friends and family at TCAC who always get their praise on!

- My immediate and extended family for all of their love and support.

- My wife, Eng, for putting up with a grumpy writer and for washing the dishes even when it was my turn. I love you.

For the past year, this book has been a labor of love. Well, actually, most of the time it just felt like labor. But anyway, these people made the ride much more enjoyable and rewarding, and I thank them for it.

Tell Us What You Think

As the reader of this book, you are the most important critic and commentator. We value your opinion and want to know what we're doing right, what we could do better, what areas you'd like to see us publish in, and any other words of wisdom you're willing to pass our way.

As the Executive Editor for New Riders Publishing, I welcome your comments. You can fax, email, or write me directly to let me know what you did or didn't like about this book—as well as what we can do to make our books stronger. When you write, please be sure to include this book's title, ISBN, and author, as well as your name and phone or fax number. I will carefully review your comments and share them with the author and editors who worked on the book.

Please note that I cannot help you with technical problems related to the topic of this book, and that due to the high volume of email I receive, I might not be able to reply to every message.

Fax: 317-581-4663
Email: steve.weiss@newriders.com
Mail: Steve Weiss
          Executive Editor
          New Riders Publishing
          201 West 103rd Street
          Indianapolis, IN 46290 USA

Preface

The funny thing about a preface is that it's the first thing you read but the last thing I write. I've been writing this book for the better part of a year, and I've had to fight through trying to maintain some semblance of a life, writer's cramp (believe me, it sure felt that way), and resisting playing Tony Hawk's Pro Skater to get this book done. You might say I was motivated.

In today's first years of the web, you might say that Internet users are motivated. They fight through slow-loading graphics, poor navigation systems, and alluring pop-under ads just to try to buy something. The battle with today's sites is to make them usable so that users who want to buy something can.

There's no argument that usability can only help improve your site. If your users can't find a product or service, they can't decide to buy it; if they can't figure out how to use your shopping cart or application form, they can't give you their business. Usability is good, but what comes next?

The answer lies in persuading the vast majority of unmotivated users to transact. There will always be those dedicated die-hards who know what they want and are determined to buy it. Everyone else, however, needs to be persuaded and supported through a decision process before they can even think about transacting.

This is a book about those decisions. It's about supporting and moving users along a decision cycle so that they are able to and want to click on that submit button. It's my hope that this book will help you to get more of your users to click.

Who This Book Is For

Web design attracts people of all kinds and backgrounds. From professional designers to the do-it-yourself business owner, everyone can benefit from learning how to make the most of the sites they design. This book was written with several types of readers in mind, and you'll probably identify with one or more of them. Pick the persona that best suits you in terms of how you should read and use this book:

- **Marketers.** You have overall responsibility for your company's web site, and you need to find ways to get more of your visitors to transact. This book will help you look at your users in new way so that you can guide them to click with you.

- **Project managers.** You recognize that you need to go beyond just delivering on time and on budget. This book will help you understand what it means to deliver the right type of content and functionality to meet your web site's requirements.

- **Business analysts.** You are responsible for defining the functional requirements of the site. This book will help you appreciate that you can't just specify separate blocks of functionality—you need to connect them together to create a seamless and guided experience for users.

- **Information architects.** As the user-experience design lead, you are responsible for structuring the site and choreographing the overall site experience. This book will show you different tactics to funnel users to transact.

- **Graphic designers.** You are responsible for the look and feel of the site—you give the site its form and its character. This book will help you appreciate design on a page-by-page basis to move users forward in their decision process.

- **Developers.** Last but not least, you are the people who create the code that actually makes things happen. This book will help you understand the importance of creating functionality that makes it easy for users to transact.

Let's Get Vertical

To provide a wide range of examples and possible applications, this book also focuses on six vertical markets. These markets were chosen based on the following:

- They are all trying to motivate users toward some call to action; if yours is a site that is simply there for people to explore, this is not the book for you.

- They are meant to cover the gamut of different types of sites. Even if your site doesn't exactly fit any of these verticals, you will probably be able to apply a combination of ideas from them.

As you read through the bulk of the chapters in this book, you'll notice some thumb tabs with icons at the side of some of the pages. These tabs represent the six verticals, and they provide a quick reference as to which vertical a particular concept is applicable to. Persuasion is highly contextual, so something that works in one vertical might not be effective in another. These thumb tabs will help you find and identify the concepts that will be of most interest to you.

This book focuses on the following six verticals:

- **Retail.** This vertical is at the forefront of persuasiveness. The retail vertical is about ordering goods online. If you're selling anything—from books to clothes to electronics—this is the vertical for you.

- **Professional services.** Lawyers, doctors, consultants, and designers all fit within the realm of professional services. This vertical is for people who sell themselves and their expertise. This vertical is about presenting a persuasive case to users that you are the right individual or organization to meet a prospect's needs.

- **Online services.** These sites provide some sort of service that is ordered or used online. The call to action for these sites is primarily to ask the user to sign up or become a member of the service. Two examples of online services are online photo ordering and web-based storage solutions.

- **Financial services.** The common denominator for these sites is money. This vertical is about providing products and services that relate to bank accounts, investing, insurance, and loans. The uniqueness of this vertical lies in the fact that all of its products are virtual (for example, bank accounts have no physical presence) and that they are heavily based on trust and security.

- **Travel.** Travel sites enable users to book a plane, rent a car, or reserve a hotel room. Travel sites are about booking short-term rentals of items located at remote places and are based on promoting convenience, safety, comfort, and leisure.

- **Marketplace.** These sites connect buyers and sellers together. Users first must be convinced to become members, and then must be able to evaluate the other party with which they are considering doing business. Career sites and online auctions are common examples of marketplaces.

Summary of Chapters

The goal of this book is to arm you with practical design ideas that you can immediately apply toward making your site more persuasive. The meat of this book discusses how to design for users depending on where they are in their decision-making process and how to move them closer to transaction.

Here's a quick summary of what each chapter will cover:

- **Introduction.** This is Persuasion 101. You'll learn the basics of how to influence users while reshaping your perspective on how web sites should work.

- **Chapter 1, "Getting Users to Click."** This chapter is the theory behind the book. It covers how users make decisions and introduces you to the four types of users featured in this book: browsers, evaluators, transactors, and customers.

- **Chapter 2, "Browsers."** These are users at the beginning of the decision cycle. They have recognized that they have a need, but they need some help to better understand what they should be looking for.

- **Chapter 3, "Evaluators."** These users want help in making a choice. They want to be able to compare alternatives, whittle down their options, and make a decision to transact.

- **Chapter 4, "Transactors."** These users have decided what and where they want transact. They need help and guidance to lead them through your call to action before they get lost or lose their motivation.

- **Chapter 5, "Customers."** These users have completed a transaction with you. They are looking to be taken care of and given a reason why they should transact with you again.

- **Chapter 6, "The Design of Everyday Pages."** Persuasion happens one page at a time, and this chapter explores the best way to design common pages that are found across all web sites.

- **Chapter 7, "Clicking It Together."** This chapter provides case studies of persuasive web sites for each of the six verticals covered in this book.

- **Chapter 8, "The Persuasive Web Design Process."** This section discusses the techniques you can use in your design process to ensure that your site is persuasive.

- **"Resources."** If you're hungry for more, this chapter has some of my favorite resources to fill your head with even more ideas.

Take It All with a Grain of Salt

As a book of ideas, *Submit Now: Designing Persuasive Web Sites* is not meant to be doctrine, and it definitely shouldn't be used as rulebook to end design debates. It is, however, a book that will hopefully inspire you to think of your own ideas.

Persuasion is an art and a science. We can draw from principles of human psychology, but the effectiveness of persuasion will depend on how we creatively seek to understand and work with the ways in which people behave. Don't let this book be the end of figuring out how to design your web site—let it be the start.

Andrew Chak
Fall 2002

Introduction

This book is about persuading visitors at your web site to do what you want them to do. It's about compelling users to add items to a shopping cart, fill out an application form, or send you an email. It's about getting users to click.

But what makes users click? There have been enough dot-bomb failures to remind us that it's hard to design and build a web site that will turn site visitors into customers. Companies now realize that improved usability can improve their transaction rates. After all, if Aunt Grace can't figure out how to check out her shopping cart, how can she buy anything?

So, in come the usability consultants (myself included) who get paid to tell you what's wrong with your site and how to fix it. Make your links blue and underlined. Make your buttons clickable. Structure your site according to how your users think. The rules, guidelines, and heuristics go on and on. Better yet, conduct some usability tests. Gather some users who match your demographic profile and ask them to perform some key tasks on your site. Measure whether or not they are able to buy a stereo on their first try and measure how long it takes to complete the task. Observe any problems they encounter, make suggestions, change the prototype, and test it again to see whether there's been an improvement. Iterate and test the design for as long as you can afford to (or until you run out of muffins); eventually, you'll have a "usable" site.

But that's not enough.

What? After all that time, effort, testing, and the numerous iterations, having a usable site isn't enough to make the site a success? Well, sure, your site should be fairly usable at that point, but there's one thing missing from the equation: Why would your users click through your site?

Just because your users *can* figure out how to do something on your site doesn't mean they *want* to. Having the most easy-to-use web site in the world does not mean people will do business with you online. You must provide more. You must create a need for your users and compel them to act. You must be *persuasive*.

A Web Hierarchy of User Needs

Abraham Maslow was a psychologist who proposed that human motivation could be explained by a desire to meet a hierarchy of needs. He suggested that people would be motivated to take care of their basic physiological needs such as food and shelter before they would concern themselves with "higher-level" needs such as being loved or having self-esteem.

The same can be said of web users. They have basic fundamental needs that must be addressed before they can be ready for the higher-level activity of being willing to transact with a site.

The web version of the hierarchy of user needs can be described in four levels:

Your site must be available, be usable, instill confidence, and create desire for your users to transact.

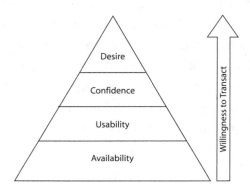

1. **Availability.** The foundation for this web hierarchy is making your site available to your users. If your site isn't reliably up, or it requires the latest browsers and plug-ins, or it feels slower than watching paint dry, then your site really isn't available for your users to use. I won't talk much about accessibility because it should be a given.

2. **Usability.** If your users can't navigate and find items, they can't purchase them. If they can't figure out how to fill out your sign-up form or check out your shopping cart, they can't transact. Usability is about users being able to use your site—especially those who are already motivated to transact.

3. **Confidence.** Web users will hesitate to transact online unless their confidence is built up in two areas: The first is the confidence that they have selected the right product or service to meet their needs, and the second is the confidence that you are the right business or organization to provide that product or service.

4. **Desire.** After you've created a site that instills confidence in your users, you need to further motivate them with the desire to transact. You have to influence your users to the point where they want to take action.

Pause for a moment and think of your own site: Is it readily available? Can people figure out how to navigate through it? Do you provide information, photos, or demos that make people want your product or service? Do you help your users feel confident that they can trust you enough to do business with you online? Do you create a desire within users that prompts them to transact? These are the fundamental elements of persuasion that will be discussed in this book.

The Obligatory Definition

Following this preamble about how persuasion is more than just usability and how sites need to meet a user's hierarchy of needs, we need a short definition of what our objective is with regard to persuasive web design. So here's the obligatory definition of what we're trying to do:

> **Persuasive Web Design:** The art and science of designing web sites that help users to make decisions that result in desirable transactions.

It's a science because repeatable methods exist to study and analyze what works on the web to define design guidelines. It's an art because the guidelines have many exceptions, and they don't cover all design decisions. Persuasive web sites guide users by providing good navigational usability, they educate users on how to make an informed choice, they allow users to be motivated by eliminating any qualms about trust and security, and in some cases, they can even move users toward a goal they didn't realize they had. In short, persuasive web sites remove barriers and motivate users toward transaction.

Seven Principles to Remember

To help set the stage for this book, I'd like you to keep in mind seven principles that I've used to design more effective and persuasive web sites. They aren't based on some massive study surveying the best practices from web developers in North America and six foreign countries. They are simply based on the practical experience I've gained during my web years.

Principle #1:
Your Competition Includes Your Competitors' Web Sites, the Web, and the Offline World

When you think about your competition, you probably will first think about your competitors' web sites. You'll compare your look and feel, your content, your functions, and even your navigation bar to theirs. Your competitors' web sites are a useful starting benchmark, but you shouldn't stop there.

One often-overlooked competitor is the web itself. Internet users seem to treat the web as one giant application. As they go from site to site, users say things like "Why isn't this sign-up form as easy as the one on Yahoo?" or "Why isn't the search on this site as quick as Google's?" Users see the web as one "thing," and they invariably will compare sites regardless of their purpose or industry. Anything short of "how good it was at that other site" might leave your users frustrated and disappointed.

The other major competitor to your site is the offline world (i.e., real life). If your site doesn't make something easier or more convenient than its offline equivalent, it probably isn't worth the disk space it occupies.

Let's compare the task of buying collectibles. Suppose I collect Beanie Babies. (Please believe me when I say that this is only an example.) In the real world, I might scour my local newspapers' classified sections in the hope of finding Poofie the Dog for sale, only to learn that the one listed seller is willing to part with only Prickles the Hedgehog. Before I despair too much, however, I could go to an online auction site such as eBay < www.ebay.com > and find 9,890 Beanie Babies available, 57 of which are my pal Poofie. In this case, the web is better at helping me find and buy Beanie Babies than the real-world equivalent.

Principle #2:
Not Everything Makes Sense to be Sold on the Internet

Okay, so this might seem like a pretty crazy guideline for a web design book, but it's true. Let's take, for example, the need to purchase dog food. If I'm going to run out of dog food in a couple of days, I conceivably have two choices:

Option 1:
Get in the car, go to the pet store, and buy an 18-lb. bag of dog food for $18.99.

Option 2:
Go online, order an 18-lb. bag of dog food for $18.99, add on $5.99 for shipping and $4.00 in weight fees for a grand total of $28.98, and hope that the shipment comes before the dog starves.

You don't have to be an animal activist to recognize the deficiency of option 2. Why would anyone choose to go online to obtain something that has a high shipping cost relative to its price and that is needed quickly? This doesn't mean that other pet-related items—such as apparel, toys, or high-margin pet products—shouldn't be sold online. You just need to make sure that your online products can meet your users' needs and that you're not catering to those who are shopping for a hungry dog.

Principle #3:
You Must Earn the Right to Transact with the User

The challenge of getting users to transact with you the first time they visit your site is like trying to steal a kiss on a first date. There's a lot you have to do before you can ask anything from your users. You need to give them something of value, and you need to prove to them that they will benefit from transacting with you.

One time I went to look at a career site (note to my current employer: I was strictly doing research for this book…), and I wanted to perform a keyword search of available jobs. Before I could do so, however, I had to register and become a member. It was obvious that the site's objective was to acquire as many registered users as possible. The problem with this approach was that I had no motivation to register whatsoever. Why should I register when I have no idea whether there are any job listings of interest to me? Why should I give my personal information to a site that has given me nothing? You've got to earn the right to ask for information or for any type of end-user transaction by first giving something of value.

Principle #4:
You Know Everything about Your Site,
but Your Users Know Nothing

When users come to your web site, all they see are your web pages. They don't know that you had to organize your site by business units because of internal politics. They don't know that because of the way that your · database was developed, you have to force them through some extra, unnecessary steps. They don't know any of these things, nor do they really care.

What your users see are the web pages in front of them at the very moment they are trying to do something. Each page either helps them move forward in the process or puts them a step back. If you have gaps in your functionality or you don't provide guidance to your users, you can't expect them to just figure it out. It's obvious to you because you've spent the past two months implementing that particular feature or section; your users, however, have just spent eight seconds on the current page and have determined that they can't figure out where to go next.

Similarly, you can't assume that your users know about your products and services. For example, some electronics sites list products according to their model numbers. This is great for the three (okay, five) people who know these numbers, but the rest of us want to find the CD player that can read MP3s. It's easy for us to know our own products and services so well that we forget how hard it was to differentiate them in the first place.

As web designers and developers, it's easy to get caught up in the internal politics and technology hurdles that narrow our vision in terms of how to design the site. It's easy for us to focus on designing a site from the inside-out, where we have great internal reasons and knowledge for why the site is the way that it is. What we must do, however, is look at the site from the outside-in. We must be vigilant and see the site from our end users' perspective to help them, rather than us, make sense of the site.

Principle #5:
Anticipate Mistakes and Variations Ahead of Time

One of the common traps that web-design teams fall into is that they focus on designing for those times when everything goes right. A design team might be working on a particular area and make statements like this: "The users will click here and enter their names, addresses, and phone numbers. They'll click Continue and then enter their user ID, click Submit, and finish the registration." Although this is fine as a starting point, you need to antic-ipate the types of mistakes and variations that users may encounter. What often happens is that the ideal situation is designed, but no consideration is given for when things go wrong.

You need to plan ahead in terms of what happens when a user doesn't enter the information properly. What if there are users from Canada? Will you allow them to register? What happens when the user enters a user ID that's already taken? Will you provide some alternative available ones? Don't wait until you're going through development to start addressing mis-takes and variations—by then it's too late. Your safety net should be con-ceived and designed ahead of time rather than trying to apply a bandage later on.

Principle #6:
Either You Do the Work or They Do It

Imagine a user named George who is going to move to a new city next month. He goes online and checks out the web sites of three banks in the new city with the purpose of determining what type of account he should open and at which bank. Here are the different experiences he might have at these sites:

Site #1

George goes to the Banking Accounts section and sees links for the Premier Account, Elite Account, and Superior Account. Hmm... he's not sure which one to pick, but he decides to select the Premier Account. On this page is a short description of the account but no pricing information. Instead, there's a link for something called a PDF that promises more detailed information. George clicks on this link, and his browser chokes because it isn't configured to read PDF files.

Site #2

George goes to the Bank Accounts section and sees links for the Basic Account, Value Account, and Premier Account. Underneath each link is a short description highlighting the main features of the account to help him select which account might be of most interest to him. Another link to Compare Accounts brings him to a page with a table highlighting the features and fees associated with each account.

Site #3

George goes to the Accounts and Account Plans section and sees the various account options. Each contains a short description, just like the second site. But a link called Choose the Right Account catches his eye. He clicks on it and sees that it's an interactive tool. It asks him about his needs and recommends an account that will minimize his fees.

These three sites are fundamentally similar in that they provide basic account information. They are vastly different, however, in terms of the effort they require of their users. George's goal is to find the right account that meets his needs. Site #1 forces him to figure out which account might interest him, but he's not helped because there are no meaningful descriptions. The web department that produced the site didn't take the time to convert the product information into HTML; they just uploaded the PDFs because it was easier for them. This forces George to work harder because he has to configure his browser to read files that were convenient for the bank to produce. Why would George want to do this?

Site #2 fares a little better by providing descriptions underneath the account links. A comparison table further helps George figure out which account is best for him, but he still needs to do some calculations to see which one is most economical for him based on his needs.

Site #3 does the most work for George. It provides all the basic information, but it also goes the extra mile by interactively helping George figure out which account is exactly right for his needs. George doesn't have to whip out his calculator, nor does he have to go back and forth between pages to compare account details.

As you progress from site #1 to #3, you see an increase in how proactive the site is in helping the user make a decision. Site #1 is definitely not the way to go because it requires its users to do too much work. Sites #2 and #3 offer two different—but acceptable—approaches that are suited to different users. Site #2 is less proactive, but it enables users to make their own informed decisions. Site #3 requires users to enter some information, but its recommendation can help reassure less confident users. Whether you would choose to implement Site #2 or #3 (or both) is up to you, but keep in mind that the more you meet your users' needs and do the work for them, the more likely they are to transact.

Principle #7:
Help Your Users Do What You Want Them to Do

This whole book is about getting your users to click. Whether it's the next link or a submit button, you need to help your users click on what you want them to click. Here's an example of a page that exemplifies this concept:

RealPlayer's upgrade page includes many redundant links to make it easy for users to choose the paid-for version of this streaming media player.

www.real.com

Okay, so you're probably wondering to yourself, "Big whoop. What's the big deal?" Well, the big deal has to do with the context of how users arrive at this page. If you were using an older version of Real Network's RealPlayer (a streaming audio and video player), you would receive a notification for a free upgrade to RealPlayer 8. When you click on that link for the free upgrade, you are brought to this page.

What's interesting about this page is the way it's laid out. The first thing you notice is all the links that say "Download Now." These links—and the one in the middle of the page called "Download RealPlayer 8 Plus Now"—all link to the Plus version of the player that is $29.95. In other words, there are four redundant, prominent links to the paid version of the application.

But where is the free upgrade? Well, it is there; it's just a little hidden. Take a look at the bottom left corner and there it is. This screen shot is what the page would look like at an 800×600 resolution, which (as of this book's writing) is still considered the minimum resolution that the majority of users have. What's even more interesting is that the link to RealPlayer 8 Basic is on the left (where people don't tend to look for next steps), and it is in a gray bar that seems to blend in with the scroll bar at the bottom.

Keep in mind that this is a very annoying page, but that's not the point here. The point is that it's obvious that Real Networks wants you to buy the Plus version of its player and that the company has gone to great lengths to make it easier for users to do what it wants them to do. I'm not recommending that you go to these same extremes, but I am saying that you need to proactively guide your users down the desired paths you want them to take.

The Stage Is Set

As web site designers, we have to realize that we need to work hard to get users to transact. We have to build web sites that are like a good salesman (minus the Vitalis) that provides the right balance of nudging and support to earn that click. Chapter 1, "Getting Users to Click," will provide the persuasion and decision-making framework to make those clicks happen.

1

Getting Users to Click

Clicking is a decision. Every click requires your users

to scan your page, move their mouse, and make a

decision to click something. Every click is a little step

of faith and a commitment to move forward.

By studying how users make purchase decisions and learning how they can be persuaded, you can gain a powerful perspective on how to design web sites that users can't resist. This chapter will reveal not only how to get users to click, but also how to get them to click on what you want them to select.

The Consumer Decision Cycle

Each purchasing decision is actually the culmination of a number of small—perhaps unnoticed—choices. For example, you've made a lot of decisions to get to this very point. First you recognized that you needed a book on how to design more effective web sites. Then maybe you drove to your nearest bookstore, headed over to the Internet section, and started scanning book covers for something to catch your eye. You probably picked up a few books, flipped through a few pages in each, and then finally decided to purchase the book you're reading right now. Each of these steps is an example of the consumer-decision cycle, and it's the cycle that all your users will go through to transact with you.

The consumer-decision cycle can be described in five different phases:

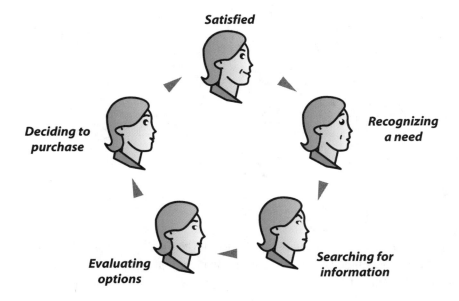

Satisfied

For users who are satisfied, life is beautiful—they have no needs and perceive that they have no problems. In an online context, these users are surfing the Net just for the sake of doing so. There isn't much you can do for these users except try to help them recognize needs they aren't aware of. In other words, show them something to interest them.

Recognizing a Need

In the second stage of the cycle, users have acknowledged that they do have a need. The problem, however, is that the vast majority of users (79 percent, according to a study conducted by Robert L. Jolles in his book *Customer Centered Selling*, Simon & Schuster, 2000) tend to be stuck in this stage and choose not to do anything about it.

Remember that annual checkup you just can't seem to get around to scheduling? Chances are, you're stuck in the "recognizing a need" stage and need something to push you into actually making the appointment. Your users, too, need help in getting unstuck so that they will take action. In other words, you need to *motivate* them.

Searching for Information

The next step in the decision cycle is the search for information. In this stage, users look for information that will help them formulate the evaluation criteria for their decision (for example, "What features should I look for in a digital camera?"). Information gathering generally takes one of two forms:

1. **Internal search.** In an internal search, users rely on their preexisting knowledge to make a purchase decision. In other words, they don't seek to gain any additional information on top of what they already know.

   This search is used for frequently purchased items such as toothpaste. In these cases, you will likely purchase the brand you bought last time (or have been buying for the past 50 times), provided you haven't had any negative experiences with it recently. Internal searches are also used for low-cost items because the ramifications for picking the wrong product or service are low.

   On the Internet, catering to internal-search products and services means providing an easy way for users to locate and identify what they have already decided to purchase.

2. **External search.** An external search involves users conducting their own research through consulting friends and families, reading third-party informational sources (consumer guide magazines and web sites), or reviewing information directly from the product or service provider.

   Users do an external search when they aren't confident about their own knowledge for a particular purchase. In these situations, you can help users become aware of needs they haven't even realized yet. These searches are also used when the risk of making a wrong purchase decision is high (for example, when buying a house).

For this type of search, your web site needs to educate your users on how to decide between their options and meet their goals.

Evaluating Options

In the evaluating stage, users whittle down their choices to a few options. At this stage, users are evaluating two things:

1. **Identifying suitable solutions.** This step involves users trying to figure out what the right solution is for their needs. This may mean deciding on a short list of products to consider, or it may mean determining the specifications for a customized solution (for example, specifiying audio/video components for a home theater system).

2. **Identifying trustworthy providers of the solution.** Another important part of evaluating options is for users to determine whom they want to purchase the solution from. It's particularly important for your company or organization to be differentiated if prospects perceive that they can get comparable solutions from multiple vendors.

It's at this point that users evaluate both the objective attributes (such as specifications and cost) and the subjective attributes (such as brand loyalty and how the product makes consumers feel). As users evaluate their possible choices, both logic and emotion play a role in making the final decision.

Deciding to Purchase

It's in the "deciding to purchase" stage that the magic happens—your users click that submit button. At this point, your users have decided that they want to do business with you (congratulations!), and now it's important for your site to focus on giving these users the confidence to follow through with their decision. After a user has made the decision to transact, the emphasis should be on streamlining the remaining steps. At the end of this stage, your users should be satisfied (provided you delivered as promised), and the cycle starts all over again.

By understanding the decision cycle, you can recognize what type of information, tools, and support you need to provide to users on your site. The goal is always to lead users from their current stage to the next stage until it results in a transaction. The momentum that propels users forward is persuasion.

Two Fundamental Motivators

Now that we know how people make decisions, we need to find a way to move them through the decision process. Motivating users is like getting a donkey to move by using a carrot and a stick. The carrot is held in front of the donkey as a potential reward for moving forward, whereas the stick is used to hit the donkey as a reminder of the punishment for not moving. So, for us humans, we can summarize our fundamental motivators as the desire for reward and the fear of punishment:

The desire for reward.

We all have a  desire to gain something or to be rewarded. This can be based on objective reward attributes (for example, the side air bags in a sports car will help protect you in a collision) or emotional ones (for example, a sports car will show others that you're young and affluent). Rewards are about communicating to users the type of person they can be or the results they can accomplish by doing business with you. That is why we will continue to have bikini-clad women selling beer for the foreseeable future.

The fear of punishment.

This is the  fear of being hurt or, more importantly, losing out on something. We humans like our freedom of choice; anything that compromises our freedom to pursue opportunities or our freedom to choose will prompt us to act. That's why discounts and coupons are set for a limited time, and shopping channels always tell us that there is only a limited number of cubic zirconia rings left. They are capitalizing on our fear of losing our freedom to choose so that we will feel compelled to act.

This understanding leads to an important insight that can give you a leg up on your competitors: To effectively reach your customers, present your product or service in terms of the rewards it provides and the punishments it helps them avoid.

Of these two motivators, however, it is more effective to emphasize the consequences (punishment) of not acting than to promote the value of what you have to offer. For example, if you were selling all-inclusive resort packages to Mexico, you might take one of these two approaches:

Approach 1: Reward sales pitch   **User's response**

This is a five-star resort on a private, white-sand beach. It has five pools, six restaurants, and great nightly entertainment. You will definitely be able to relax and do a lot of sightseeing at this resort.

Hmmm… that sounds pretty good. I'll think about it and get back to you.

Approach 2: Punishment sales pitch   **User's response**

This is a five-star resort on a private, white-sand beach. It has five pools, six restaurants, and great nightly entertainment. You'd better book your ticket soon, however, because there are only a few rooms left. It is so popular, the price might even go up.

Okay, here's my deposit. Please reserve a spot for my wife and me right now.

The reward approach emphasizes the benefit to the recipient, but it doesn't motivate the person to transact. The punishment approach, however, forces the vacation shopper to respond immediately. As you design your web site, always think about how to incorporate these two fundamental motivators to move users forward.

The Six Elements of Influence

Influence is the umbrella term for persuasion. Influence is about changing a person's thoughts, feelings, or behaviors. Persuasion is about influencing people in such a way that you gain their compliance without exerting force.

The Internet is a medium in which users truly are not forced to do anything (unless you count closing those annoying pop-up ads). In the real world, a salesperson might use persuasion techniques to get you to buy something, but in the online world, there is no person for users to feel accountable to. What you can do, however, is take the best elements of persuasion and apply them as web-design principles.

One of the foremost experts on persuasion is Dr. Robert Cialdini (author of *Influence: The Psychology of Persuasion*, William Morrow, 1984), who spent countless hours observing, training, and participating in sales for everything from encyclopedias to portrait photography to dance lessons. He also worked in advertising, public relations, and fundraising agencies to learn their techniques for persuading people to respond positively.

One of his key findings was that we tend to take a number of mental short-cuts to arrive at decisions. When we're presented with these shortcuts, we respond to them in an automatic fashion, like reflexes.

Dr. Cialdini illustrates this through the story of a sales clerk who accidental-ly doubled instead of halved the price of turquoise jewelry that was selling poorly. Tourists often frequented this store, and when the price of the jewel-ry was doubled, the items started to sell out! What happened here was that the tourists used the mental shortcut that said "expensive = good." They weren't necessarily knowledgeable about jewelry, but they probably figured that "you get what you pay for" and opted to purchase what they perceived to be higher-quality pieces of jewelry. It is by leveraging these types of mental shortcuts and their automatic reactions that we can design persuasive web sites.

In our everyday world, we are constantly subjected to persuasion techniques. How often have you bought something on vacation only to regret it later? How many times have you bought something because you felt bad for the salesperson? Have you ever bought something because someone else told you it was good? If so, you've already come in contact with (or fallen victim to) some of the persuasion techniques discussed in this section. Here are the six key elements of influence that you can use to change the behaviors and attitudes of your web site visitors:

- Scarcity

- Commitment and consistency

- Reciprocity

- Social proof

- Authority

- Liking

Let's explore each of these in more detail.

Scarcity

Scarcity is a widely used compliance tactic, yet we fall for it all the time. The premise behind this element of influence is that we believe that things that are scarce are worth more than those that are widely available. That's why rare items such as misprinted stamps or *Revenge of the Jedi* posters are deemed to be more valuable. Make something scarce and people will want it all the more.

Let's compare the posters for two high-school raffles to see how scarcity can be effectively used:

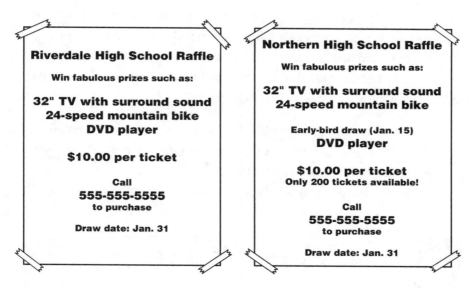

In this case, both schools happen to have the same prizes and draw date. Riverdale High School presents all of the relevant information in a clear, straightforward manner, but there is no urgency to act. Northern High School's raffle poster is much better because it takes advantage of scarcity. First, there's a scarce number of tickets—only 200 are available. This immediately conveys to prospective buyers that the tickets are worth more because there are a limited a number of them, along with the fact that the odds seem better. Second, there is a limited-time offer for the early-bird drawing for the DVD player. This again promotes scarcity because the early-bird drawing is available only to early ticket purchasers.

When it comes to your web site, how do you promote scarcity? Do you provide limited-time offers? Do you tell prospective buyers that there are a limited number of products available at a special price? Do you feature exclusive items that only you have available? The more scarcity you feature in your site, the more people will want what you have to offer.

Commitment and Consistency

One of our core values is that we want to remain true to our word. We don't like to be caught contradicting what we've stated before. If you ever want to lose weight, one way to do so is to tell all your friends and family that you intend to lose 20 pounds by the end of the year. The fact that you've externally committed to this goal will be a strong motivator for you to be consistent with it and get on that treadmill.

In a persuasive context, the idea is to get prospective buyers to commit or agree to easier items up front and then ask them for a more difficult commitment at the end that is consistent with the upfront commitments. Here's an example of someone soliciting a donation:

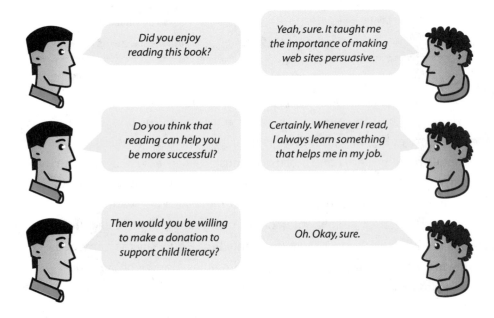

The way this technique works is by asking for easy commitments up front and then closing with what you want your prospects to commit to at the end.

On the web, commitment and consistency are about asking users to commit to smaller decisions up front and then asking for larger commitments later. Take, for example, the sequence in which e-commerce sites ask users for information when they are checking out their shopping cart:

As you progress from left to right in the preceding example, the questions become a little more committal. It's easy to ask users to verify their shopping cart items. Asking them to provide a shipping address is a bit harder, but it makes sense given the context of the task. Selecting the shipping method is more committal because it involves selecting an option that involves a cost. Finally, asking for payment information is the hardest to do, but because the user has already come this far, he or she is more likely to commit to the transaction.

Reciprocity

Reciprocity is the old "give and take" in which you give something to a prospect only to ask for something in return. Reciprocity is based on an ingrained concept of obligation—if someone gives you something, you're obligated to reciprocate in some way. The power of this technique for you as a web designer is the fact that you, as the giver, can control what you give your customers, and you can specify what you want from them in return.

The principle of reciprocity might not be quite so compelling on the Internet because people don't feel any obligation toward web sites. Specifically, the way the principle applies online is that the site has to give value before the user is willing to give anything of value (in this case, personal information) in return. Let's see how this works through two site scenarios:

Site #1

Gerald is looking for a job as a financial analyst. He goes to a job web site that he saw advertised and decides to start his search there. He clicks on the search function, but instead of being presented with a search field box, he is asked to register and upload his resume before he begins using the site. Gerald becomes frustrated; he doesn't know whether he should bother registering because he doesn't know if this site has any job listings that are relevant to him. In the end, Gerald decides to leave.

Site #2

Leann is also looking for a job, and she is interested in making a move up in her accounting career. She goes to a job site that a friend told her about and clicks on the option to search. She scans through the search results and reviews a couple of the job postings in detail. She sees one posting that catches her eye, and in order to upload her resume to the employer, she decides to register with the site.

Functionally speaking, these two job sites are the same. The sequence in site #2, however, is much more successful because it gives the user some value before it asks for anything. On the Internet, giving something of value to the user is not just a requirement—it's a prerequisite for users to even consider dealing with you.

Social Proof

The influence of social proof is based the assumption that because everyone else is doing something, it must be either good or right. If you go to a busy intersection and stand looking up into the sky, chances are others will do the same. If you see someone on the street asking for help, and everyone else is walking by, might you choose to ignore the person as well? Social proof allows us to reason, "If it's okay for them, it must be okay for me."

The Amazon.com web site is a textbook example of using social proof. In the following quick snapshot of a book's main product page, you can see many aspects of social proof in use:

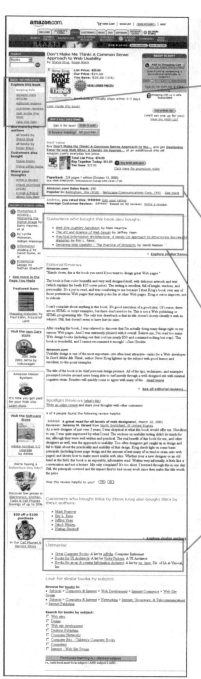

Customer Reviews

These are the thoughts and opinions of people who have read this book.

Amazon.com Sales Rank: 190
Popular in: Bellingham, WA (#18) , Netscape Communications Corp. (#9) , See more

Purchase Circles

This displays groups of users in which this book is popular. For example, this book is popular with employees from Netscape.

Customers who bought this book also bought:

- *Web Site Usability Handbook* by Mark Pearrow
- *The Art and Science of Web Design* by Jeffrey Veen
- *Practical Information Architecture: A Hands-On Approach to Structuring Successful Websites* by Eric L. Reiss
- *Designing Web Usability : The Practice of Simplicity* by Jakob Nielsen

Customers Who Bought This Book Also Bought...

This provides a list of books that people who buy this book also tend to buy.

Listmania!

- Great Computer Books: A list by jeffofla, Computer Enthusiast
- Books for UI Architects: A list by Vicky Pickens, A UI Architect
- Books for an up & coming Information Architect: A list by viz_dave, Dir. of IA at Vizooal, Inc.

Listmania

These are personal lists of recommended books created by Amazon users.

Amazon.com provides a great example of how to "prove" to users that they'll like a particular book by showing what others think of the book.

Authority

We have a natural disposition toward authority—it's part of the way we've been brought up. Listening to an authority we respect is an easy way for us to make decisions. We hear references to authority every day, such as "Ebert and Roeper give this movie two thumbs up!" or "Four out of five dentists surveyed recommended this mouthwash." Deferring to authority makes it easier to decide because the decision is made for us.

Epinions < www.epinions.com > is a site that is all about establishing authority. Epinions is a consumer buying guide in which members contribute their own product reviews. For this site to be effective, it must establish its members as authorities, and it does this by providing each of them with a profile page:

Each Epinions member has a profile that summarizes the number of reviews he or she has written, as well as the number of members who have voted to "trust" this person for his or her opinions.

www.epinions.com

Two key elements are used to establish a reviewer's authority. The first is the Web of Trust on the left. As users navigate through the site, they can choose to vote for reviewers whose opinion they trust. These reviewers will gain more credibility and authority as more users vote for them. The second element is the Activity Summary on the right, which helps give reviewers credibility based on how many reviews they've written and how many visitors have viewed them.

Your site can take advantage of using authority by providing expert opinions on the products and services you provide. You don't have to have a famous authority to provide an opinion; instead, you can simply present information from your own experts. By taking steps to present these experts as being credible, you can make it easier for your users to choose to listen to them.

Liking

If you have the freedom to choose between salespeople, you're more likely to give your business to someone you like. Good salespeople will go out of their way to make you like them. They'll try to find something in common with you or to discover a means to compliment you to get you to like them and to get your business.

The principle of liking can be extended online in two ways:

1. Liking the web site itself

2. Liking the company behind the web site

Liking a web site is a very subjective matter. Every user has his or her own preferences when it comes to colors, navigation, and even the attitude of a web site. If you do have a target audience in mind, you should design according to its tastes to increase the likelihood that it will like you.

Liking a company is also a subjective matter. In this case, however, liking will be based on things such as the company's background, its values, and how it contributes back to society.

Ben & Jerry's "Give a lick!" section on their web site tells you about the social programs they are involved with, giving customers even more reasons to like them.

www.benjerrys.com

How the Web Is Different

The elements of influence discussed in the preceding sections give you good insights into how to persuade people to act. Despite the cliché, however, the web is different. The web is unique because it is an interactive medium in which users have the control. As we design for this relatively new medium, we must understand the context of how users interact with the web.

Users Can Go from Start to Finish

One of the empowering capabilities of the Internet is that it can support users throughout the decision cycle. Users can identify their needs, learn about products and services, investigate details, and execute a transaction without having to drive, phone, or sign a check. The expectation for users is that a web site should be able to help them no matter where they are in the decision-making process.

Users Go Online with a Purpose

Booz-Allen & Hamilton and Nielsen/NetRatings[1] conducted a study that introduced the concept of *occasionalization*. This term refers to segmenting users not by their demographics, but by the tasks they want to accomplish during their visit. In other words, we shouldn't be defining our users strictly according to their age, occupation, and shoe size. Instead, we should define users by whether they are at the site to browse or they know what they want and want to transact right away. By designing your site to enable your users to find what they need at their particular decision stage, you can be more effective in meeting their needs and converting them into customers.

The Internet Doesn't Have Any Salespeople

Users don't usually feel bad about staying on a particular web site for a long time, but they certainly feel that way if they've asked a salesperson for a lot of help without buying anything. There is no sense of guilt on the Internet because there's no one to feel directly accountable to. Whereas a department store might train its sales staff to be more effective at persuading customers to buy, a persuasive web site needs to provide the content and tools to help users convince themselves that they should buy.

Designing for Decisions

One of the greatest misconceptions about web sites is that they're about selling. This is completely wrong. If there's one statement that summarizes what this whole book is about, it's this:

On the web, you don't sell to people; you help them to buy.

---

[1] For more information, go to: http://extfile.bah.com/livelink/livelink/76803/
?func=doc.Fetch&nodeid=76803

The paradigm shift here is that the most effective sites don't focus on coercing users to transact. Rather, they focus on enabling users to persuade themselves and make decisions. It's a slight nuance, but it's an important one to recognize.

From the users' points of view, the best web site is one that enables them to make informed decisions. The efficiency of the Internet as an information-distribution network creates an expectation in users that they should be able to make better decisions by going online. Your site should be more of a helping tool than a selling tool. By getting behind and supporting your users, your site will be much more effective than if you try to pull them along with a sales pitch.

Make Decisions Easy

To be decision friendly means to make it easy for your users to decide between options. Imagine yourself going to a computer retailer's web site and being presented with the following choice of computers:

ECS P3-800	ASUS P3-933	ThunderBird 1.4G
ECS motherboard	ASUS CUV4X-E ATA100	ASUS a7VE ATA 100
128MB PC133	256MB PC133	256MB PC133
10GB 5400r/1.44	20GB 7200r ATA100 HD/1.44	30GB 7200r HD/1.44
40X CD	8/4/32 CD-RW	16X DVD
S3 16M AGP	TNT2 32M 4XAGP	G-force 2MX 32M
56K Modem	10/100 Network / 56K Modem	10/100 Network/ 56K Modem

Which one would you choose? If you're an avid computer user, you probably understand what the descriptions mean, but you'd still have to do a considerable amount of thinking as to which system would be appropriate. Compare this with the following alternative versions:

Basic Online	Home Office	Serious Gamer
Pentium 3 800MHz	**Pentium 4 1200MHz**	**AMD ThunderBird 1400MHz**
This basic system has everything you need to get online. It features a 10GB hard drive, which is more than enough to handle word processing and MP3 downloads. It also has a built-in modem that makes it easy for you to get online.	This system will help you be more productive at home. A large 20GB drive gives you lots of space for advanced applications and storing your files. Built-in ethernet networking makes it easy to connect to other computers or the Internet.	This powerful system will just blow you away. The 16X-speed DVD and 32MB video card give you the raw horsepower for dazzling onscreen graphics at high resolutions.

The second set of options makes it much easier for the user to choose. The first set describes the computers in terms of their specifications; the second set describes them in terms of their use and their benefits. It's much easier to differentiate between the Basic Online system and the Serious Gamer than to differentiate between an ECS and an ASUS a7VE motherboard. Don't just dump your product specs online and make your users work to figure out their choices—present your information in such a way that it makes it easy for your users to decide.

Simplify the Options

Another way in which decisions can be made difficult is by providing too many options to choose from. Let's go back to the vacation package example. Suppose you've just arrived at the travel agent's office and are beginning investigate your options:

What vacation packages do you have available?

We have 376 vacation packages all over the world. Here are the brochures. Let me know when you've decided on one.

As ridiculous as this example sounds, it does happen. In fact, it happens on a lot of web sites that treat themselves as database dumping grounds with large, overwhelming catalogs of products. The problem isn't listing all of these products; the problem is that many sites don't provide any guidance to help users sort through the listings and determine the best candidates to meet their needs. Giving users too many options can force them into decision paralysis and prevent them from being able to make a decision at all.

Remove Decision Barriers

Users enter your site at different stages in their decision processes, and one of your objectives is to remove whatever barriers might stand in the way of them taking the next step. If there are known concerns about your product or service, you need to address these head on. If there are deficiencies, you need to address them and provide users with perspective.

Suppose you were in charge of marketing the iMac computer at Apple. The greatest opportunity and the greatest challenge would be to convince existing PC users to even consider buying it in the first place. To get to this point, you must confront their concerns up front, as in these two examples:

Concern: Do Apple computers have enough software?

Response: There are more than 2,500 applications for the Macintosh, including popular applications such as Microsoft Office and Adobe Photoshop. You can also run Windows software using an emulator.

Deficiency: Doesn't the all-in-one enclosed form factor make it difficult to upgrade?

Response: Everything you need to surf the Internet, edit movies, and connect to other peripherals (such as your Palm Pilot) is already included. If you want to, you can upgrade the memory as well as add wireless networking later on, and it's easy enough that you can do it yourself.

You wouldn't necessarily quote these concerns or deficiencies in your marketing or web site material, but you'd make sure to include the information in the responses to allay your prospects' concerns up front. By proactively addressing these roadblocks, you can provide the proper perspective (the one you want your users to have) and bring them one step closer to transaction.

Removing decision barriers also happens at the site level, specifically in terms of security and privacy concerns. Whenever you ask your users to submit any personal information or conduct a transaction, you need to give them reassurances that it is safe to do so.

www.bn.com

Barnes & Noble's "Add To Cart" button has text beneath it to reassure users that they can always make changes to their order. The link to the "Safe Shopping Guarantee" also helps alleviate any concerns users might have in purchasing items online.

Provide the Right Information at the Right Time

The decision-making process is one that generally follows the same sequence time after time. Users might vary in the amount of time they spend in each stage, but their sequence of steps essentially will stay the same. Given that different users approach your site at different stages in their decision-making, the challenge becomes providing the right information at the right time.

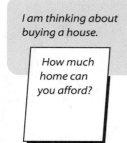

I am thinking about buying a house.

How much home can you afford?

I need to find a mortgage.

Understanding mortgage options.

I want to apply for a mortgage.

What you'll need to apply.

I've applied for my mortgage what's next?

How to look up your application status online.

In the above example for a mortgage site, users that are at different stages in their decision-making process require different pieces of information.

To provide the right information, you need to map out the information requirements for your product or service in each decision stage. For example, people applying for a mortgage need to know what type of mortgage to get and, before that, how much they can afford. How do you know what each user needs to know at each decision stage? One approach I've used is to think of four different types of users who represent how your site will be used from a decision-support perspective. Let's take a look at these four users now.

Designing for Four Users

Designing your web site can be simplified by keeping in mind just four types of users. These users represent people's different needs as they move through the decision-making process, as in the mortgage example just mentioned. Any step in the decision process can happen online or offline, so it's important that your site be designed to cater to each of these four users throughout your site.

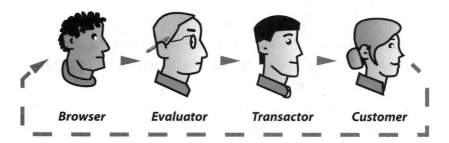

The next four chapters of this book deal with designing for each of these users and moving them along to the next step, but first, here's a brief introduction to each of them.

Browsers

Browsers don't know exactly what they want, but they do recognize that they have a need to fulfill. At this stage, browsers are looking for information to help them better understand their needs to provide a context for decision-making.

Evaluators

Evaluators have gained enough knowledge to be able to compare their options. They go to your site for detailed information about products and services. Their objective is to be able to select a product or service and the provider from which they want to buy.

Transactors

Transactors have made a decision, and hopefully, they've decided to buy something from you. For these users, you want to provide an experience that feels safe but that also speeds them through the transaction process before they are distracted from closing the deal.

Customers

After your users transact with your site, they become your customers. The goal here is to ensure their satisfaction and ease the path for them to transact again.

I use these users to evaluate how well my current or proposed site meets the needs of each one of them. Do I have something on the site that draws browsers in? Do I make it easy for evaluators to inspect product details? Can transactors buy something right away if they already know what they want? Do I have site features that help make my customers more loyal? By catering to these four users, we can ensure that we are creating sites that accommodate users at every stage of the decision process in order to move them closer to transaction.

The next four chapters will go into designing for these users in detail.

2

Browsers

The web attracts many people who utilize it in a variety of ways. The first type of user is the browser. These aren't software browsers like Netscape or Internet Explorer; rather, they're users who are just starting to look for something. They've recognized a need in their lives, and they're looking for a starting point that will lead them to their goal. They don't necessarily know what they want, but they have arrived at your site like someone at a store's window display—looking for a reason to go in.

Browsers might be first-time visitors looking for more information about your company, or they could be people just thinking about making a major purchase. Maybe they're looking for a gift for a friend. In any case, browsers are looking for something to catch their interest.

When browsers arrive at your site, they are like tourists—they generally look lost, need assistance, and are trying to find a way to fit in. The first step in moving these browsers along their decision cycle is to help them find what they're looking for or what they *should* be looking for to meet their needs.

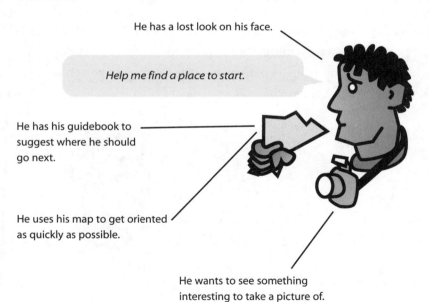

He has a lost look on his face.

Help me find a place to start.

He has his guidebook to suggest where he should go next.

He uses his map to get oriented as quickly as possible.

He wants to see something interesting to take a picture of.

In the real world, if you don't get to see the product, you're *not likely to* buy it. On the Internet, the reality is harsher—users who can't find it *can't* buy it. Unlike tourists, Internet users don't have a tour guide or a guidebook to tell them that they should be able to find what they're looking for.

The primary objective with browsers is to guide them to where they need to be. Internet users are like men who drive, get lost, and don't ask for directions. I've observed many users who absolutely believe they are in the right place for something that is actually in another section. Despite my failed attempts at telepathy, these users refuse to click over to that other section where they'll find their answer. You need to anticipate the variations in how users might choose to access your site and make it easy for them to get back on track. If you don't, your users will become lost, get frustrated, and assume that the product or service they're looking for doesn't exist.

In designing for browsers, you need to know the three different ways in which these users want to move through your web site:

1. **Wandering.** These browsers have come across your web site with no real purpose in mind, and they are looking for a reason to click into your site. These users are explorers who are looking for something interesting to catch their attention.

I'm just surfing; show me something interesting.

2. **Finding.** These browsers are looking for something specific. They might not know exactly what they want, but they are looking for some help to find it.

I am looking for a gift for my mother.

3. **Learning.** These browsers are novices who want some background information and educational material so that they can start forming evaluation criteria and be knowledgeable enough to understand more complex products. They want to find information that is provided to them in an intuitive way, yet they need to be engaged.

What do I need to know about mutual funds?

This chapter is about drawing browsers into your site. The emphasis will be on designing your home page, navigation, and search functions because these are the primary tools for browsers to find their way into your site. If you help these users find something, they'll stay; if you don't, they'll get lost.

Introduce Yourself

Retail

Professional

Online

Financial

Travel

Marketplace

> ### Overview
> Your home page should quickly identify who you are, what you do, whom this site is for, and what the user can do on the site.

Most web sites are rude. They just expect you to arrive at their home page and figure out what they do. The problem is that they don't take the time to introduce themselves.

Do you know what Buydig.com sells? How about Chumbo.com or Sparco.com? They all sell computer-related products, but you wouldn't know this just by glancing at their names. With so many domain names already registered, companies sometimes have to resort to having a less-than-ideal domain name that might not clearly identify the company or what it does. That's why all web sites must, in some way, introduce themselves.

Your web site's home page is where it gets introduced. This is where the first impression is formed so that users know what to expect and how to interact with your site.

At a quick glance, your home page should introduce the site by answering three questions:

Your web site's home page should provide an introduction in four ways:

1. **Show your logo.** As obvious as it sounds, your logo tells your users that they are at the right site, specifically if you have an offline presence. This is especially important if your company's URL isn't www.company.com (at least in North America) or if your organization's URL isn't www.organization.org. Having a clear, clean logo on your site is like an official seal that establishes the identity of your site.

2. **Include a tagline.** Unless you are McDonalds, IBM, or Coca-Cola, you'll probably need a quick tagline or description to explain what your web site or your company does. This description should either be near your logo or be a prominent statement in the middle of the page. This description isn't necessarily your slogan, but it should be a concise and functional explanation as to what you do.

   Here are some good and not-so-good examples of taglines:

   The Good   **"Enabling the cost-effective delivery of broadband services everywhere."** This is an effective tagline because it explains what the company does, but it also communicates the business benefits that it provides. This company doesn't just deliver broadband services; it delivers them cost effectively, and they are able to deliver them everywhere.

   Not Bad   **"Empowering communications service providers with comprehensive eBusiness support support-system solutions."** This tagline isn't bad because it is straight to the point in describing what the company does. The only minor criticism is that it's a little cluttered with a couple of multi-syllable buzzwords. (Oh well, you can't win them all.)

The Ugly   **"Where laziness is your friend!"** This is an example of a too-cute-for-its-own-good slogan being used as a tagline. This tagline does absolutely nothing to explain what the company does (it's for a site that helps to organize Internet-based tools such as email and online calendars), and it makes me wonder what other personal attributes that I can start considering to be my friends.

3. **Be picky about your images.** The web site equivalent of "You are what you eat" is "You are what your pictures are." When visitors arrive at your web site's home page, your pictures convey a lot about what your site is. Depending on how you choose your pictures, you might either attract or alienate your target audience.

One question that users ask themselves is "Does this site reflect who I am?" One way for users to draw a conclusion is by looking at your site's pictures. When testing a financial web site a couple of years ago, I watched users shy away from images that didn't look like them. One particular site had a predominant picture of an older woman, and it proved inviting only to older women. The first thought that a number of users expressed was "That doesn't look like me." People wanted to see themselves in the site. If the financial institution intended to attract an older, female audience, this would be fine; otherwise, many users were being alienated.

The same also goes for pictures of products. For example, if you are having a sale on women's clothing and decide to feature a few of these items on your home page, new users to your site might think you only sell women's clothing even if you are a department store. You need to be picky about the images you present and make sure they help your users understand the full scope of products you offer.

DeliverAll	SEARCH [ ] GO

Shop | About Us | News | Customer Service | Privacy Policy

Antique white panel bed.
4865 $299.00

Free Shipping on All orders over $300.00 before tax.

Welcome to **DeliverAll.com**. Our goal is to provide you with a one-stop Web shop for all of your home furnishing needs. We pride ourselves on selling quality furniture and accessories for the home and office at great prices. Our goal is to get your furniture order set up your home in four weeks or less. You can feel confident ordering at **DeliverAll.com**. Our friendly customer service staff is available for assistance five days a week and all items on our site come with a 30-day satisfaction guarantee. While you're here, why not take a look at our large selection of hand painted furniture? You'll also find an array of lamps and paintings to brighten any room. Our plush velvet sofas add a soft touch to any living room and our leather sofas are priced well below the competition. Look around and if you can't find something on our site, feel free to contact us and we'll assist you in any way that we can. Our Commitment to you: great furniture, low prices and friendly, reliable service.

www.deliverall.com

DeliverAll.com's home page features a picture of one of its beds. This prominant photo might mislead some users into thinking that this site only sells beds. Another problem is that the links to the main sections are hidden on the next page after the user clicks on this bed. The risk here is that new users might not be interested in this bed and will go away before clicking on it to find out what this site has to offer.

4. **Don't hide your main sections.** Your main sections are the infrastructure for your site's organization, and they provide a means for your users to understand what your site offers. Users who see main sections such as Hardware and Software will have an easier time figuring out that they are at a computer store, regardless of the domain name. The trouble, however, is that some sites hide their main sections. Here are some do's and don'ts for showing off your main sections:

- Do display your main sections above the screen fold—this is the area of a web page that is presented to users without them having to scroll.

- Don't clutter up your home page with special features at the expense of visually obscuring your main sections.

- Do display your main sections on the first page that your users see on your site. Don't force users to click through to another page to hunt for your main sections.

- Don't hide your main sections in a drop-down menu. If users don't click on the drop-down menu, they will never realize that there are main sections to navigate through.

The combination of images and the prominent display of main sections clearly communicates what users can buy at the Williams-Sonoma site.

www.williams-sonoma.com

Support First-Timers

> **Overview**
>
> If your site is an online service or a marketplace, you should explicitly support your first-time visitors to attract more users. Corporate and information-oriented sites should be self-explanatory without an explicit guide.

Although the days of dot-com Super Bowl commercials have mostly passed us by, a considerable amount of money is still spent on advertising and promoting web sites. The next step is to convert these media-sent browsers to dedicated users. An effective way to convert these browsers is to support them as first-time visitors.

Online

Every new user who visits your site is going in cold, so you have to provide these visitors with a warm welcome to get them started. These users are looking for welcome mats that read something like "first-time users," "learn more," "how it works," or "getting started." Like a good host, you need to invite these users in, make your introductions, and get them mingling.

Marketplace

Taking Care of Warm Users

Sometimes your users are warm ones—that is, they've come to your site because they've received a flyer or they saw a magazine ad. For these users, you need to make sure that they find a meaningful entry point on the home page that relates to what they saw offline. This could mean repeating a key phrase or using the same visual so that users can easily identify the related web site area.

These guides are particularly important for web sites that are an electronic exchange or an online service; new users are the lifeblood for these sites' ongoing growth.

The objective of a first-time visitors' guide is to show users what they can do and how they can do it. Don't waste time explaining how the site functions because this should already be self-evident. Your users should be learning how to order prints from their digital photos or how to find the right gift for their 7-year-old nephew, not how to use your navigation system.

Provide a Tour

eBay's success correlates to its user base. More users translates to more buyers, better auctions, more sellers, more products, and more revenues. To grow its user base, eBay prominently displays a section on its home page to help new users become oriented on how to use the site.

eBay provides a tour to help new users become familiar with how eBay works. Orientation tours such as this one are effective in helping users become more productive faster.

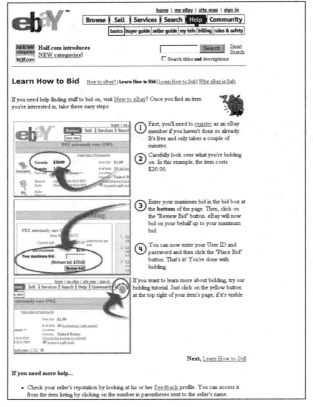

www.ebay.com

Here are some principles to keep in mind when you are developing a site tour:

- **Focus on users tasks.** The main sections of eBay's tour focus on the questions "How do I bid?" and "How do I buy?" Only the essentials are covered to get visitors using the site as soon as possible. Resist the temptation to show off the latest and greatest features and functions that you've added to your site. New users aren't interested in your bells and whistles; they just want to accomplish their goals.

- **Provide visual references.** Don't just talk about an essential feature or section—show it. By including screen shots, you make it easier for your users to recognize where they need to click, rather than forcing them to remember.

- **Include direct links.** When you discuss a particular feature, provide a direct link to it. Some users will go back to the tour a few times and might use it as their primary navigation. Think of your tour as an essential version of your site map, but with some instructions and explanations.

- **Address any issues or concerns up front.** eBay's tour includes a "Why eBay is Safe" section to address any security concerns. Features that protect eBay members from fraud and security risks are highlighted. The objective here is to put any concerns to rest so that new users will have the confidence to join and use the site.

Expose the Black Box

One of the concerns that users might have regarding web site interaction is that the site might feel like a "black box" where users don't have a concept as to how the site works or how it provides its services. Snapfish is an online photo processor that takes either regular film or uploaded digital photos, prints them out on photographic paper, and delivers them to you. One of the prominent areas of the site is a "learn more" section that includes a flowchart outlining how the process works.

The "How Snapfish Works" page helps users understand what happens to their rolls of film after they send them in.

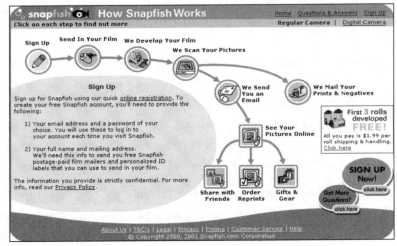

www.snapfish.com

By exposing (sorry for the pun) this process, Snapfish is building trust with its users. Explaining the process helps set user expectations and also gives users a process to hold Snapfish accountable to. By understanding the process, users can explicitly know what will happen to their roles of film so that they can feel confident enough to send them in.

Provide Multiple Paths

> **Overview**
>
> Enable your users to access information or products through multiple paths. Don't force them to think according to how you want to structure your web site.

Retail

Professional

Online

Financial

Travel

Marketplace

No matter how you design your site, different users will want to navigate your site in different ways with the intent of reaching the same destination. A left-brained person might find that funky lamp in Lighting > Desk Lamps, whereas a right-brained person might look in Urban Style > Lighting. Having a site structure in which each product or service is only accessible through one path can lead to many users not being able to find what they're looking for. The success criteria for browsers is that they must be able to find what they want regardless of how they get there. Your site needs to be flexible in allowing users to find their own way through the site; otherwise, you might risk losing them.

Door Number One, Two, or Three?

The KBkids web site enables users to enter via multiple entry points. The left hand navigation column on the home page enables users to shop by age, price, brand, and category.

These multiple navigation paths are essentially predefined product searches, but they do the job by enabling users to shop in whichever way they feel like. These entry points let users navigate according to their current mind-set, rather than imposing a one-size-fits-all navigation structure on the users.

Multiple entry points (found along the left side of the page) enable KBkids users to navigate according to their current mindset.

www.kbkids.com

Being at Two (or More) Places at the Same Time

Another way to provide multiple paths is for the same product to reside in multiple locations within the site. If you were to look for a pair of Airwalk One skateboarding shoes at Fogdog Sports < www.fogdog.com >, you might find them through the following navigation path:

Home > Footwear > Skateboarding > Casual Skate Shoes >
Airwalk One Skate Shoe

This seems pretty logical, and many users might choose this path. Some users, however, might be attracted by the link to the Skateboarding section featured on the home page. These users can also find the same shoe, but their click path is slightly different:

Home > Skateboarding > Footwear > Casual Skate Shoes >
Airwalk One Skate Shoe

It's the same shoe with two different paths and two different users who found what they were looking for. Neither path is more "right" than the other, but the more paths you provide, the greater the likelihood that your users will be successful in finding items of interest on your site.

Bottom-Up Pathing

A final example of multiple pathing is at the online bookseller Fatbrain. If I were looking for an HTML guide and ended up at Lynda Weinman's book about creative HTML design, I would see a collection of subject categories related to this book at the bottom of the page. These links implicitly say to me, "Did you find what you're looking for? If not, try one of these related links." Instead of providing me with the paths from the home page down, I now have quick access to related sections from the bottom up. Again, it doesn't matter how your users get to the right page, but it does matter that you provide your users with related links from wherever they are.

The section category links at the bottom provide related paths to find what a user might be looking for.

www.fatbrain.com

Search and Ye Might Find

> **Overview**
>
> Most internal web site search engines are rendered useless because they rely on automatic indexing to return results. Useful searches require human intervention to properly map search queries with meaningful search results.

Retail

Professional

Financial

Travel

Marketplace

There are two types of search engines: useful and useless. Some searches help, and some hinder. How many times have you gone to a site's search engine only to end up getting lost and frustrated? Web navigation can be a challenge for some users, so they see a search engine as a lifeline. As their search queries return meaningless results, however, they feel like they've been given a pair of cement boots.

The Evil All-Text Search

Most web site search engines are rendered useless because their content is automatically indexed. One of the easiest ways to implement a search is to have a spider crawl through all the pages of your web site and take note of all the words on each page. When a user enters a search term, the search engine looks for the pages that contain the greatest number of instances of that word and then prioritizes them in the results. This is what I refer to as a useless search.

> **Useless search:** A form of search engine that produces results based on an automated spider crawling through pages. This is likely to lead users to irrelevant links based on what they were originally looking for.

Searching is not a word popularity contest. If I go to the Compaq web site to search for a Presario computer, I get relegated to the bowels of the press release section because these pages contain more recent mentions of the word "Presario" than elsewhere. Hasn't it occurred to Compaq that I might be looking for a Presario computer? Searching is about helping users find things and is not about automated document indexing.

The search results for
"presario" include 774
pages, the first of which is
a press release. How lovely.

www.compaq.com

All is not lost, however. Although automatic indexing might not be that smart, real humans can do a pretty good job of it. Useful searches require human intervention to intelligently understand the search term and subsequently guide users to the right result.

Useful search: A form of search engine that has been intelligently rigged by a human being who anticipates how people enter search queries and then leads them to the most likely place that will help them find what they're looking for.

Keyword Versus Full-Text Searches

Most users have no concept of the difference between a keyword search and a full-text search. Keyword searches work by assigning keywords to each page in your site. When this search is executed, only the documents that have been assigned the keyword are returned. Full-text searches simply search the entire page for any matching terms and return those. Most users expect searches to behave like a keyword search, but many sites use a full-text search (which requires less work to implement) that ends up frustrating users with too many results.

Rigging Your Search

Rigging your search results is not about cheating your users. Instead, it's about providing the most useful set of search results that will lead users to what they're looking for. The way you rig your search is through a process known as *keyword mapping*.

The way this works is that you look at your search engine's log files and look at the most popular words with which your users are searching your web site. Then you map these words to the pages that are most relevant for that search term. The search results at Microsoft's web site provide users with a list of Best Bets that are the "rigged" results for a given search term.

The search results for "video games" on Microsoft's site provide meaningful links to topics such as downloading the latest release of DirectX and the official Xbox site.

In general, you should rig your search results so that they lead to the best general overview page for that particular topic. In the Microsoft example, the "Best Bets" links are to the main section pages for those particular products rather than a sublevel page. This enables users to see an overview and to drill down to where they want to go.

Can You Spell "Fritillaria"?

Russ Brown from Userlab < www.userlab.com > once told me about his quest for fritillaria flowers at the GardenWeb site. He went to the site and typed in a search for "fritalarea," and despite his misspelling, he was given the right results. I myself tried "frittallerea," "frittallarea," and even "frittleria," and they all yielded the same correct result. GardenWeb's search has properly anticipated the fact that most people don't know how to spell plant names and has made it easier for users to find the right plants. Correct spelling shouldn't be prerequisite for making a purchase or finding a result.

GardenWeb's search engine is a forgiving one that matches incorrect spelling with the right results.

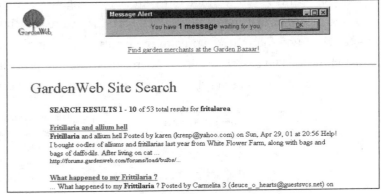

www.gardenweb.com

You should keep in mind spelling variations for your product names. Just because you know how to spell your product names doesn't mean your users do. Again, you should take a look at your search-term logs for the creative spelling variations that your users enter and map those terms to the relevant results.

Provide Specialized Searches

Although a keyword search is the most common and probably the easiest for people to understand, it isn't necessarily the right type of search for all types of products or services.

The iQVC shopping site provides the expected keyword search, but it also has some additional interesting search options. The power search enables you to search via description, brand, price, or item number. The fashion search enables you to find clothing by apparel type, size, and color. The jewelry search helps you find pieces by size. If you're looking for something blue for a new bride or if you want to see the availability of style of ring by finger size, you're in luck. Strictly relying on a keyword search might not always be the best way for your users to find what they're looking for.

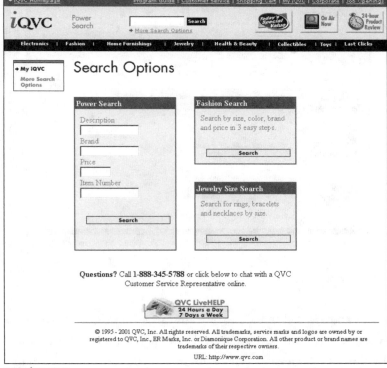

iQVC's specialized searches help users get to the right products faster.

www.iqvc.com

Moviefone sells movie tickets online. To generate revenues, the site needs to help moviegoers find movies, and it does this very well through its searches. Moviefone provides five different searches, and they each provide a different way to help users find a movie that they might want to go and see.

Moviefone's movie search makes it easy for users to figure out what they want to see.

www.moviefone.com

Moviegoers who know which movie they want to see can search by title. Those who want to base their decision on what's playing around the corner can search by theater. Moviegoers who want to see whatever movie is popular can search through the current top 10 movies. Users interested in seeing a particular genre of movie can search by type. Those who perhaps saw a movie trailer that featured a particular actor but don't remember the movie's name can search by the star. By providing all of these search options, Moviefone goes beyond just providing a search. The site is helping users *find* a movie to watch.

Product Versus Information Searches

One thing to keep in mind is that when users enter a search term on your site, you cannot assume they are looking for a product or service. Instead, they might be searching for information about that type of product or service. Remember that browsers haven't necessarily decided on a particular product that they are looking for; they are just starting in their decision process.

At the SmarterKids web site, the search results by default display product matches, but users can also click on the Information tab to view related articles on that search topic.

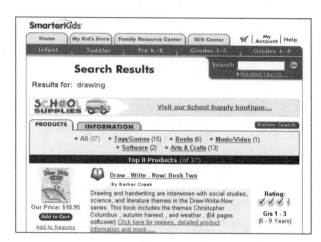

Users who search for "drawing" at the SmarterKids web site are given search results for both products and informational resources related to the topic.

www.smarterkids.com

Provide Easy Starting Points

Retail

Professional

Financial

Travel

Marketplace

> **Overview**
>
> Some users don't know what to buy and require some initial suggestions to get started.

I hate gift shopping. I especially hate trying to buy for a Christmas gift exchange because I always end up with someone who I don't know that well. It's a pressure-filled situation—I have to buy within a fixed amount of time within a designated budget while not resorting to purchasing a hula-hooping Santa Claus doll as a gag gift. The same can be of any type of purchase—sometimes we just don't know where to start. It's at this point that we need sites to provide us with some suggestions to get us going.

Popularity Counts

The influence of social proof is that people believe that whatever everyone else is doing is also good for them. An easy way to get people started into your site is to list the most popular items.

hifi.com has a "Help Me Choose" page that acts as a start page to help users choose an electronics item to purchase. One of the links on this page is to the Popular Products area where users can see what others are buying. Users who view popular items will probably say to themselves, "Hey, these are pretty popular; they must be good buys," and are inadvertently influenced.

Bring in the Experts

Your site is expected to be an expert in the products or services you sell. hifi.com provides a section called "Ask Kate" in which she provides her expert opinion on selecting audio/video components. To make such a section effective, you need to establish your expert's credibility by including a bio or background information. A variation of this approach is to provide staff recommendations for your products or services, which hifi.com also provides through its "Stuff We Love" section.

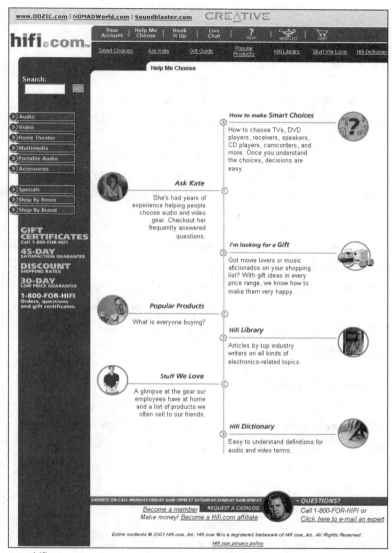

www.hifi.com

hifi.com's "Help Me Choose" page helps users get started on finding something to buy.

An alternative (albeit more expensive) approach is to feature an already-well-recognized expert. This approach provides your site with a credible opinion that might also be perceived as a more objective.

Finders Keepers

Finders are interactive tools that ask users a few questions to provide some recommended solutions. The most common form of finder is a gift finder like the one included in the hifi.com site. Finders usually ask a few short questions (Who is this gift for? What is your price range? What types of interests does the recipient have?) to arrive at a list of gift ideas.

Finders are an important tool because they are for users who don't know exactly what they're looking for. When users use finders, they are asking the web site for its recommendations based on their input.

One finder that I really like is Quicken's stock search. (What they've labeled as a search function in this case really behaves as a finder because the results are generated based on user preferences and not a direct query.) A stock finder enables users to enter in their preferences (show me all U.S. small cap stocks that have a share price of less than $5.00) to find stocks. Quicken's stock finder provides some good options to consider when you design and implement your own finders.

Provide Prepackaged Options

Finding stocks can be a tricky proposition. To make things easier, Quicken has packaged together the most popular combinations of user parameters and lists them as Popular Searches. This is useful for a user who doesn't want to think about the details and wants to quickly find some recommendations for common types of stocks.

Quicken provides prede-fined searches to make it easy for users to start searching for stocks.

www.quicken.com

The Step-by-Step Interview

The interview version of a finder asks users for their preferences one question at a time. Quicken's EasyStep Search provides full explanations for each of the questions asked. This approach helps users understand the options so that they can become equipped to find stocks on their own.

The EasyStep Search guides and educates users through the options so that they can learn to do their own more advanced searches.

www.quicken.com

Full Control Finding

Don't forget to provide an alternative for your advanced users as well. Quicken provides a Full Search option that displays all of the different variables; this enables advanced users to have direct control over the finder.

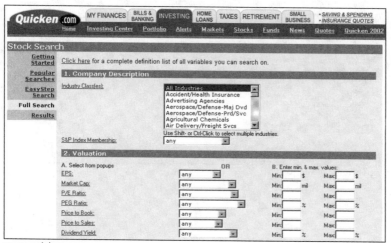

For the control freak in all of us, Quicken offers a full search that enables users to enter more than 30 different variables.

www.quicken.com

Be a Matchmaker

In some cases, a specialized type of finder called a *matchmaker* is the only meaningful way to find products. This is useful for users who have existing products and are looking for items to add on to them.

Crutchfield is an electronics store that sells car-audio components and features a matchmaker. One of the neat features of the site is called "What Fits My Car?" This finder asks you to specify the year, make, model, and body type of your car to find compatible car-audio components. When I enter in my 2000 Honda Civic coupe, I find out that the Aiwa CDC-MP3 will fit my car. The site also automatically remembers my car selections so that the next time I return, my car will be a prepopulated selection.

Now, whenever I go to any other car-audio site that doesn't have this type of finder, I will feel very insecure about making any purchase before consulting Crutchfield's site. This finder has become a must-have tool for me, and it will always bring me back to this site whenever I am considering car-audio components. It's this type of compelling functionality that can make finders a competitive advantage.

Crutchfield helps me find the car-audio components that fit my specific car.

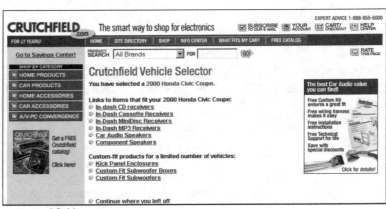

www.crutchfield.com

Don't Forget the Date

Overview

When users come to your web site during certain significant dates or times of the year, you can use that as a context for better customizing your site to your users.

Retail

Professional

Online

Financial

Travel

Marketplace

In December of 1999, I noticed some interesting changes that Amazon.com < www.amazon.com > made to its home page as Christmas drew nearer. Like a web site voyeur, I took some screen shots to track the changes, and here's what I observed.

December 20

www.amazon.com

At the top of the main content, the user is greeted, and a link to ordering deadlines is featured because there is still time to have gifts delivered before Christmas. The main feature on the page is the "Editors' Choice" section to help shoppers quickly decide which gifts to buy.

December 23

www.amazon.com

A few days later, a link to gift ideas is still provided along with information about ordering deadlines. However, email gift certificates are starting to be promoted as a last-minute alternative.

December 24

www.amazon.com

It's now Christmas Eve. It's too late to ship gifts in time, so there are no more gift ideas or ordering deadlines. Instead, email gift certificates are now prominently featured as a last-minute gift.

Do you know what was featured on December 25? A feature on how to redeem and use gift certificates, of course!

What Amazon.com has so cleverly demonstrated is an understanding of how to use dates as a context for customizing the site experience for users. People who are shopping the site in November and early December can afford to take their time. Last-minute shoppers using the site in late December need to know ordering deadlines and quick gift suggestions. Shoppers coming in on Christmas Eve need email gift certificates as a lifeline. We all live in the same calendar year, so users who are surfing your site on a given date can tell you something about their potential interests.

It's Not Just About Christmas

The same concept can apply to other times of the year just as easily, such as Valentine's Day, Mother's Day, Father's Day, and Secretary's Day. But don't limit this idea to just gift-giving occasions and e-commerce sites. How about accounting sites during tax season? Or official movie sites leading up to and after the premiere? Time is a context that we all share, and we as designers can use it to better connect with our users' needs.

Another way to adopt this idea is to look at times when your site might not be as busy. Historically, Tuesdays have been the weakest night for movie theaters, and that has lead to the creation of "cheap Tuesdays" at some theaters. In the same way, you could examine when your site receives less traffic and offer a discount for orders made during that time period. Amazon.com has begun to feature Friday specials, perhaps to stimulate sales on what might otherwise be a slow day. Time might equal money, but on the web, timing can be just as equally important.

Teach and They Shall Follow

Retail

Professional

Online

Financial

Travel

> **Overview**
>
> For some products and services, your users will need to learn before they can buy.

Before I began investing in stocks, I invested in mutual funds. Before mutual funds, I had certificates of deposit (CDs). Before CDs, I had my checking account, and before that, I had my piggy bank. My investing-and-saving strategy has changed over time, and this has correlated with my level of financial knowledge. It wasn't until I understood the basics of risk and return and how the stock market worked that I ventured beyond CDs and checking accounts. In the same way, for some products, a certain amount of knowledge needs to be gained by users before they can even consider purchasing those products. That is why we need to provide learning materials on our web sites.

Educating your users can help put you in a place of trust with them. If you allow your customers to be educated elsewhere, you run the risk of losing the relationship. Users who learn at other sites might choose to make the purchase with the information source they trust.

This section covers a few reasons why it is important to include learning material with your site.

Creating the Need

Do you have tornado insurance? I don't, and I don't know many people who do. But what if you were to move to a farm in Oklahoma? Would you then buy tornado insurance? The fact that I'm asking might get you started thinking about it. But if I were to tell you that Oklahoma is located in Tornado Alley and has one of the highest occurrences of tornadoes by state, you might become quite inclined to purchase tornado insurance.

In this case, the need for tornado insurance was created based on the fact that you learned something. Without this learning, the need never existed. Providing the appropriate learning material can help you create the need within your users for them to consider purchasing something they hadn't previously thought about.

Enabling Users to Decide

A lack of knowledge can lead to insecurity, and this can lead to an inability for users to decide. I recently had some laminate flooring installed in my back room, and like a wannabe do-it-yourselfer, I headed over to the nearest home-improvement superstore to look at some options.

As I was pacing up and down the laminate flooring aisle, the only useful comparison I could make was in price. I had no idea, however, why some flooring was $1.49 per square foot and others were $4.00. I assumed that there was some difference in quality, but I was not sure of the benefit. I was stuck and couldn't decide what to get.

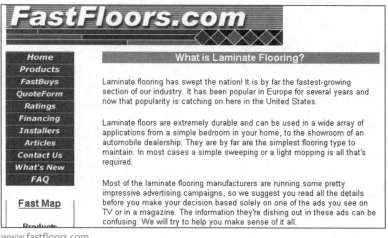

FastFloors.com helps users understand the differences between laminate floor options.

www.fastfloors.com

When I asked the salesperson for some help, he explained to me that some flooring could be installed without glue for faster installation and that some are more resistant to water than others. He provided the learning material I needed to be confident enough to make a decision. Good learning material will educate your users on the factors they should use to evaluate their options.

Get 'Em When They're Ready

Sometimes users just aren't ready to go forward. They might need some time to think about things, or the timing just isn't right. In any case, you want to establish your site as a reliable and unbiased information resource that users can return to when they're ready.

The idea is to demonstrate to users that your site has useful content and resources so that when they're ready to proceed, they'll start by coming back to your site.

Allow for Bookmarking

Overview

Make it easy for users to bookmark any page in your site to motivate them to return later.

Retail

Professional

Online

Financial

Travel

Marketplace

Sometimes your users just aren't ready to take the next step toward making a transaction. In these cases, you can still provide a valuable service to your customers by enabling them to bookmark or reference the page that they're on. This section will discuss three ways to allow your users to bookmark your site.

Allow Users to Bookmark in Their Browser

This is the easiest and most obvious way for users to bookmark information. To support this, you need to make sure that the URLs to your pages don't change.

If page URLs do change, you need to provide a redirect or some capability to track down that page. The only disadvantage with relying completely on browser bookmarking is that you have no means to track how many times a page has been bookmarked.

To facilitate browser bookmarking, you need to make sure you have descriptive titles within your HTML pages. The page title is what gets displayed in the bookmark list, and it should include your site's name as well as a description for the specific page. Another caveat is that you should avoid using frames in your site because some older browsers have a difficult time properly bookmarking them.

Email It to Yourself or a Friend

This is an increasingly popular feature on both e-commerce and content web sites: Users can enter an email address to which the URL of the current page can be sent. This is particularly helpful when more than one person is involved in making the purchase decision.

If I am in the process of purchasing a dishwasher, I am going to want to send my wife the link so that she can evaluate the product. All I have to do is type in her email address, and the link is automatically sent to her. This is more convenient and fail-safe than requiring me to compose a new email in my email program, type in my wife's email address, and then copy and paste the URL into my message. This feature is also useful when the two decision-makers are geographically separated.

Maytag's web site allows me to email a product page to my wife, my friends, or even myself.

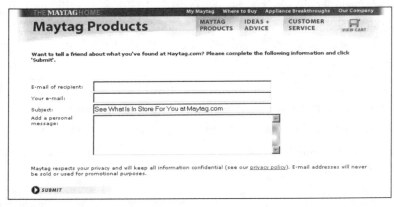

www.maytag.com

Another reason to provide this functionality is for users who happen to be surfing at work. Sometimes if I come across an interesting product or article, I'll forward that page to my email at home so that I can review it after hours. (Yes, I know. The life of a writer can be a lonely one.) This helps me keep my work and personal information separated.

The advantage of this technique for the web site designer is that it enables you to track which pages are truly popular. Pages that are forwarded to others carry an implicit stamp of approval saying, "This page is important and relevant enough to be forwarded on to someone else." If you use only page hits as a measure of popularity, how are you going to differentiate between pages viewed out of interest and those found by people getting lost?

Save It on the Site for Later

Another variation of bookmarking is the capability to save the product or content directly on the web. On e-commerce sites, this is commonly referred to as adding something to your wish list. It's like placing something in a temporary holding area until you decide to place it in your shopping cart.

This is perhaps the most complicated and advanced way to implement bookmarking. Although you do gain the benefit of being able to track user interests, many users might not choose to use this function because it usually requires registration. In the case of e-commerce sites, some users can become confused when they place items in the wish list, thinking that they are putting something in their shopping cart. So you need to weigh the benefit of this functionality with the complexity that it adds.

Home Depot's web site enables its users to bookmark renovation resources in a personal area called "My Projects." After users register for the service, they can surf the Home Depot site and add content to their personal area for future reference. This helps create a sense of ownership within the site, and it encourages users to return and use the site as a resource for future projects. Allowing users to save information for later can give them a reason to come back.

The "My Projects" list on the left side of the Home Depot site stores links to additional ideas for projects you may want to try in the future.

www.homedepot.com

3

Evaluators

As you learned in the preceding chapter, a

browser comes to your site just beginning to look

around, window-shopping to see whether you've

got anything worth sticking around for.

Evaluators are people with more intention:

They are the ones who make decisions while

they're at your site.

This chapter focuses on the techniques you can use to help evaluators make the decisions you want them to make on your site. Evaluators need to decide which product to buy, whether they should use your service or whether they should contact you.

Evaluators are like investigators: They collect the facts, analyze them, and draw a conclusion. If you saw an evaluator in a store, you'd see him or her pacing up and down the aisles, scanning the products. These users pick things up, try them on, and read the back of the cereal box. They are users who want to buy, but they'll only do so after they're satisfied that they've made the right choice.

Help me decide.

He carries a checklist of key criteria.

He has done some background research to help him make an informed decision.

He has a magnifying glass to check out the details.

He has comfortable shoes and is willing to walk around to find the information he needs.

Evaluation on the web can be difficult. This two-dimensional medium provides information only through text, graphics, and some sound. Users can't touch, smell, or taste products, or get a sense of the people providing a service. As a designer, you must overcompensate for the web's inherent weaknesses and create an online experience that makes it easy for your evaluators to transact. The only way to do this is to provide the right content.

The right content helps users experience your products and services as fully as possible—it's the next best thing to being there. Content should convey how soft the bed sheets are, how great the jogging shoes fit, and how happy users will be when they use your company's services. If you don't provide the content to help your prospects experience what you are offering, you can't expect them to do business with you.

Content should also overcome objections. Thoughts like "Does this really meet my needs?" or "It's too expensive!" or "I don't trust this site enough" must be overcome before the user will click to submit. For evaluators, you need to remove any barriers and doubts that might prevent them from clicking with you.

Evaluators will use your web site in three different ways:

1. **Selecting.** These evaluators need to understand and evaluate their options, and want to pick the right product or service that meets their needs.

2. **Designing.** These evaluators have specific needs and need some help to design a customized solution.

3. **Judging.** These users need to feel confident in doing business with you—whether it's buying from you or hiring you for your services.

You can help evaluators make the choices you want them to make by giving them the content and tools they need. The sections that follow show you how to do just that.

Differentiate Between Products

Retail

Professional

Online

Financial

Travel

Marketplace

> ### Overview
>
> Your users aren't part of your marketing department, so don't expect them to know the differences between your products. Differentiate your products with supporting descriptions or accompanying images.

One of the first things that evaluators will encounter is a list of your products or services. The problem with many web sites, however, is that they fail to differentiate the items listed on the page. This forces users to navigate up and down between pages until they find the right one or decide to go elsewhere.

How to Tell Two Brothers Apart

To illustrate the importance of differentiating between products, let's look at a comparison between Brother's Canadian and American web sites for listing their laser printer products.

First let's look at the Canadian site.

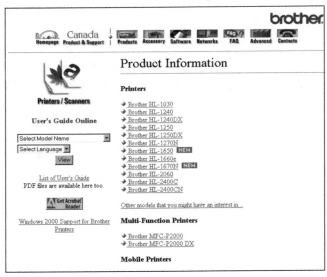

www.brother.com

The simple listing of product numbers as hyperlinks seems innocent enough. The assumptions here are that users are looking for more information on a specific model and that they know its model number. But what if they are looking for a small workgroup laser printer that can be easily networked? Where would they start? They might start by clicking on the first product, scanning its content, determining whether it can be networked, and if not, clicking back to the product listing and looking through another product. These innocent-looking links are creating a lot of hard work.

A few users might be persistent enough to click through all the product links, but many will not. Most of these users will leave this site not knowing whether there's a small workgroup laser available that can easily be networked.

Now let's look at the American site.

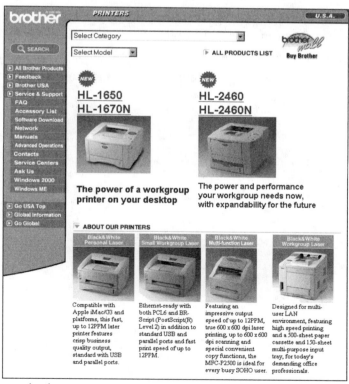

www.brother.com

The difference here is simple—as you scroll down the page, there's a section called "About Our Printers" that labels laser printers according to useful categories such as "Black & White Personal Laser" and "Black & White Small Workgroup Laser." This helps the user find the right laser printer without having to worry about model numbers.

This concept is applicable to any site that has a list of products and services. Don't expect your users to know the differences between your bank account types, service packages, or product names.

Use Pictures to Differentiate

The Gap's web site provides a useful approach for differentiating its various styles of men's khakis. When you first go into this section, you're presented with a list of links to pant styles such as "lightweight clean-cut khakis" or "relaxed fit flat-front khakis." This provides quick access for people who already know the Gap's khaki styles. For those who don't know the difference, however, they can choose the option to "View As Images" to differentiate between the styles. The elegance of this solution is that there is a default text view that is quick for familiar users, and there is also an alternative image-based view that is helpful to new users.

Know your khakis? If you do, the default list view (to the left) is fine for you. If you don't know the difference between "easy fit" and "relaxed fit," however, you can get a quick idea through the images view (at the bottom).

www.gap.com

It Starts with Great Content

Retail

Professional

Online

Financial

Travel

Marketplace

> **Overview**
>
> Compelling content is the key to getting users to buy.

Selling products is the ultimate goal of most transactional sites, but to sell, you must convince your users to buy. Aside from the appropriate photos (see the next section), the essential ingredient for compelling users to click on that button is your written content. This is where the sale is made or broken. This is where users decide.

The key to compelling content is to write from your users' points of view. Why should they buy the product? What are their needs? What are their concerns? The key word here is "benefits." If you describe your product in the context of what's in it for your users, they will be more inclined to bite.

Even though content is extremely important, it is often taken for granted. We're often more interested in designing the rollovers for the navigation bar or putting the content into a database. We also usually repurpose existing content with the assumption that it's already "good enough" to make the sale. You have to remember, however, that on the Internet, your users aren't in a showroom; they aren't holding the product in their hands, nor are they able to smell how fresh it is. Your content needs to explain clearly how your product gives users what they want.

Products Are More than Just Features

One of the easiest ways to describe a product is by highlighting its features. Although this is a useful start, don't forget the other side of the equation—benefits. Consider the following two options for product copy describing a stereo:

Option 1: Features Only

Main Features

- Front tray loading CD player

- Digital AM/FM stereo tuner

- Cassette deck

- Full-function remote control

- Backlit LCD display

The preceding option is short and sweet. It simply tells users what the features are and lets them get on their way. For some users, however, this product description might be unsatisfying, and it definitely isn't compelling. Users might ask themselves, "So what?" and move on.

Option 2: Features and Benefits (Taken from 800.com)

Main Features

- **Front tray loading CD player** slides out for fast-and-easy access to the CD, plus it reduces space requirements.

- **Digital AM/FM stereo tuner** processes FM and AM radio broadcasts digitally, locking in on the signal for less drift and reduced distortion. It also allows for simple storage of station frequencies in convenient presets.

- **Cassette deck** allows playback of cassettes in the handy built-in mechanism. Cassettes are still the most popular playback and recording format in the world.

- **Full-function remote control** provides complete control of the unit from the comfort and convenience of your chair.

- **Backlit LCD display** clearly shows you important information, even in low light.

Option 2 is much more compelling because it explains how the features are related to the benefits. For example, the front tray-loading feature reduces space requirements, and the digital tuner enables you to store presets. For users who are questioning the need for a cassette deck, they are reminded that cassettes are still the most popular playback and recording format used. The preceding description is also just as quick to scan as option 1 through the use of bolding the features. An alternative version of option 1 would be to link from each of the features to an explanation of the benefits. By explaining how features translate into benefits, users are given more information to be able to decide in favor of purchasing this product.

One more point: Make sure you start with the most important user features and benefits first to grab the user's attention, and then work your way down the list.

Address Concerns Up Front

Are there any doubts or reassurances that your users will need regarding your products? If so, you need to be proactive and address these concerns up front. Just think about how your customers will thank you if they find this type of information at your site and not your competitors'.

Addressing these concerns at your site will help position it as a reliable information resource that should be consulted prior to making any purchase. Let's take a look at a description of a tie-dye product that used to be on the eToys web site.

This product description for a tie-dye kit helps address any concerns. One improvement, however, would have been to rearrange the paragraph into bullet format to make it easier to scan (as in the previous example with the stereo).

Now let's take a look at the concerns that someone might have as he or she decides whether or not to purchase this product:

Concern	Reassurance
Will it make a mess?	"The dye comes in squeeze bottles so that you can control where the dye goes." "Rubber gloves are included."
Will the dyes run in the wash?	"Soda Ash Dye Fixer keeps the colors even through the washing machine."
Do I have use up all the dye in one sitting?	"The dye can be used for up to two weeks after it is mixed."

This product description has incorporated the likely obstacles that users might have to overcome to decide on this product. Without these reassurances, the user might never be comfortable purchasing this product.

Disclose Weaknesses with Perspective

This point is a touchy one—companies generally don't like to disclose product weaknesses. With the wealth of information available on the Internet, however, and the capability for discussion groups to share feedback, it's quite possible that your prospects will discover these product weaknesses anyway. In this case, you should be proactive and disclose any perceived weaknesses so that you can provide the proper perspective to your users. For example, computers that don't come with floppy drives are described as "legacy-free" and are promoted as being easy to set up and support via a network. CD boom boxes that don't come with cassette players can emphasize their smaller size and relative lightness. Users expect web sites to divulge both positive and negative information, but the silver lining is that you have the opportunity to frame the situation to your advantage.

Provide Factual Product Detail

The advertising great David Olgivy once said, "The more informative your advertising, the more persuasive it will be." With this thought in mind, you need to make sure your site provides the informative details that users expect to find.

Some tips to keep in mind as you develop your product details are as follows:

- **Don't be afraid to go long.** In other words, don't go short on the details. There will always be users who have very specific questions that they want your web site to answer.

- **Don't be modest.** This isn't a recommendation for you to be conceited about your products or services, but you should make sure you cover all of the relevant features and benefits that they provide.

- **Don't overwhelm your users.** On the flip side of the first point, don't just dump all of your content for your users to wade through—organize it. Break up your content into subsections to make it easy for users to find the details they're interested in.

- **Write for a specific person.** Try to imagine a specific person who is representative of your target audience. What would this person be interested in? What issues might be important to this person? Write your content with this person in mind.

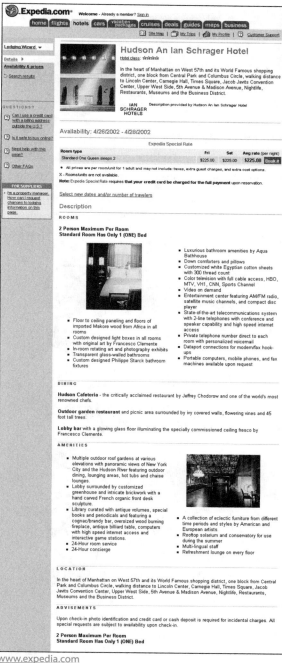

Expedia.com has detailed hotel information listings (that usually are provided by the hotels themselves). By reviewing this hotel's information, I was able to find out that each room has HBO and a CD player, and that the hotel is within walking distance of Times Square. If another hotel had the same features but didn't describe them in the details page, I would never know that they existed and consequently would be less likely to choose that hotel.

Retail

Pictures That Sell

> **Overview**
> High-quality images that help evaluators examine your products can give you a competitive advantage.

In the offline world, evaluators pick things up. They open product packages, hold items up to the light, try them on, and sometimes make quite a mess. On the Internet, however, the only thing your users can pick up is their mouse. Photos give you a way to overcome this physical limitation. Pictures help evaluators visualize your product and answer questions like these:

Travel

Show the Details

Many web sites are designed as if they were newspaper flyers in which every product only gets one photo to sell itself. Web sites aren't limited by a desire to save paper, however, so they should provide as many photos of a product as possible.

A while ago I was interested in buying a computer bag, but I didn't want something that looked like a computer bag because I was afraid it would become a target to be stolen at an airport. Given that I was looking for something a little more casual, I tried looking at the Altrec site. I took a look at the Trager Cross Country Laptop bag, and this is what I saw:

Hmmm… looks like a pretty simple bag. I wonder how much stuff you can put in it?

www.altrec.com

There's nothing wrong with this photo, but there also isn't much to get excited about. The bag just looks like a bag.

But what if I were to wander over to eBags's site? The Trager bag is featured as one of the best-selling computer bags, so I decided to take another look. This time, this is what I saw:

This looks like the same bag, but it's got something different. These additional photos look like I can click on them.

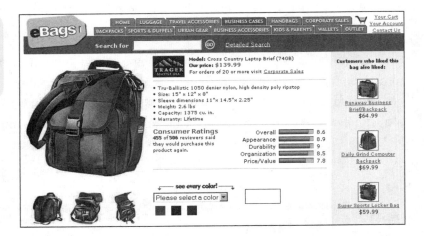

Hey! I didn't know that it could be converted to a knapsack. Cool!

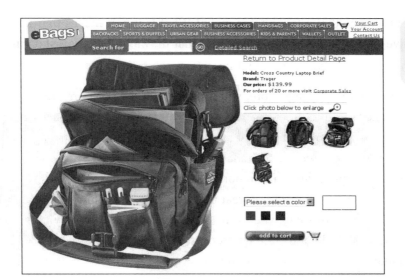

Good. It's got lots of compartments. There's even one for my mobile phone.

A-ha! I see the laptop sleeve and it's padded. Wow, it looks great—I want this bag!

www.ebags.com

Lands' End's virtual model lets users see how outfits might look on them.

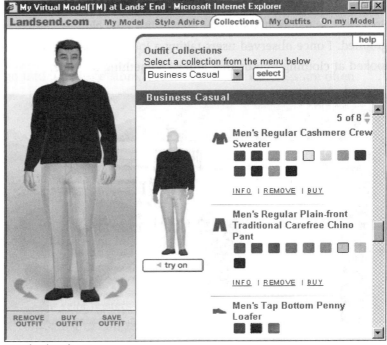

www.landsend.com

Sometimes Drawings Are Better

Photos are usually helpful, but sometimes drawings can be even better at communicating details about a product design because they eliminate distracting visual details. Here's an example from Franklin Covey's web site with an appropriate use of drawings to sell binders:

The simplified drawings on Franklin Covey's web site help highlight the differences in binder designs.

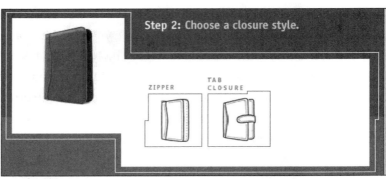

www.franklincovey.com

Let Your Users Do the Talking

Overview

Use the testimony of your users to provide a credible review of the products and services you offer.

Retail

Professional

Online

Financial

Travel

Marketplace

Have you ever bought a book because a friend told you it was good? How many times have you watched a movie because it received a good review in the newspaper? How about choosing a doctor based on a personal recommendation? When it comes to making a lot of our decisions, the best opinion is often someone else's.

One of the most effective ways to persuade someone to buy a product or service is to present someone else's opinion of it. User reviews leverage elements of social proof and authority and can present a compelling case for users to consider purchasing a product or service.

User-Generated Reviews

User-generated reviews enable your users to contribute their own reviews about the products you sell on your site. By allowing users to contribute, they take more ownership of your site and can become more loyal.

For this type of review, you should provide the capability for users to assign an overall rating to the product. Ratings allow for an aggregate rating based on all of the customer-contributed reviews and make it easier for your users to get an overall sense of the reviews. It's also important for you to explain what the ratings mean and what the scale is. (Don't you just hate it when you see a movie rated as four stars and you wonder whether the rating was four out of four or four out of five?)

When users contribute their reviews at KBtoys.com, they are given an explanation as to what each star rating means.

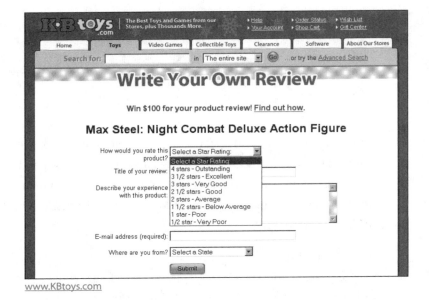

www.KBtoys.com

When it comes to displaying your ratings, make sure you indicate the scale they are based on. The star ratings on the left don't tell users whether it's three out of three or four or five!

Don't do this: ★★★   **Do this:** ★★★☆

It's also important that you include some sort of user identification. This is where you allow reviewers to include selected details about themselves (such as where they live, what they do, and so on) so that readers have some assurance that the reviewers are real people. This also provides some context behind the reviewers' comments.

Amazon.com takes a further step in giving credibility to reviewers by having the reviews rated as to whether or not they are helpful. This helps encourage reviewers to write useful reviews, and it can be a means to automatically prioritize the most helpful reviews.

External Reviews

External reviews are an appeal to authority. External sources such as newspapers and magazines are seen as being able to provide expert and objective views about your product. To give these types of reviews greater credibility, make sure you fully reference the reviewer and the source publication. You might even provide a direct link to an online version of the review so that users can choose to verify the content.

Prewritten Testimonies

This last type of review is most applicable to companies that sell a service. In this case, the company interviews a customer and writes up a testimonial about that customer's experience. Given that your company writes these reviews, users might become suspect of the information provided. To overcome these doubts and create a believable testimony, you should feature the customer as much as possible. Include the name and a photo of your customer and any other relevant details, such as where the person lives or what he or she does. Quote your customers so that they do the talking for you. The implicit statement here is that these customers really stand behind their comments—even to the point where they would feature themselves in the testimony.

www.broadvision.com

BroadVision features a "What Customers Say" section that literally allows its customers to do the talking through video testimonials of their experience with BroadVision's software.

One other idea worth mentioning is what Net Perceptions (a software company) does with its customer testimonials. Although the company quotes its customers much like everyone else, it establishes greater credibility by quoting its customers from external publications—sort of a combination between an external review and a testimony. Again, the implicit statement here is that the customer is happy enough with the product he or she is willing to provide a quote about it in an objective, third-party publication.

Net Perceptions provides customer testimonials through quoting its customers from external publications.

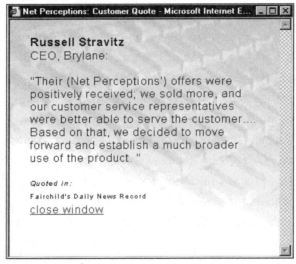

www.netperceptions.com

Comparing Apples to Apples

Overview

Comparison tools help your users learn about key product or service features, and give them the confidence to make a decision.

Retail

Professional

Financial

Travel

Comparison tools enable users to place products or services side-by-side to compare their features. Comparison is one of the essentials of evaluation, and it provides users with the assurance that they have done their due diligence in making the right choice.

Product and service comparisons do the following:

- They enable users to see a summary of multiple options all at once.

- They highlight what the important product or service features are.

- They highlight the differences that might not otherwise be noticed.

- They provide an opportunity to up-sell customers to a higher ticket item or service than they originally intended.

Comparing Products

You'll use this comparison when you have a set of products or services that are fairly similar and need to be differentiated. A good example of this is the Gap's "compare fits" tool. This tool helps business-casual professionals understand the differences between the various shapes and styles of the Gap's khaki pants.

This tool is particularly noteworthy because of its visual nature. The user can view and compare pants from the front, side, and back views. Another interesting feature is the sketch view that highlights differences in the cut of the pants that might otherwise have been difficult to notice through the photos.

Gap's "compare fits" tool enables you to see pants from multiple angles and includes a sketch view that emphasizes the differences in fit and style.

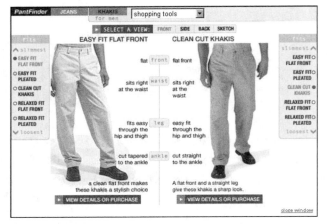

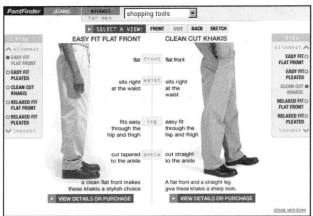

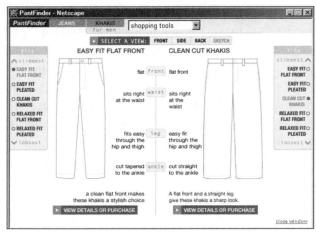

www.gap.com

Comparing with the Competition

This comparison is used for comparing your products or services with your competitors'. Your challenge is to present a comparison that positions your product in the best possible light while trying to appear objective.

Mercedes-Benz does a good job of this when it uses comparison information from a third-party source. This is an indirect way for Mercedes to say, "Even though you're on our web site, we're going to give you an objective comparison of our cars versus the competition."

One advantage of this approach is that you get to control the checklist of items for comparison and thus the sales pitch. The objective here is twofold: to place your product in the best possible light by highlighting your best features and to prevent the user from feeling the need to visit other sites (especially your competitors') for further information.

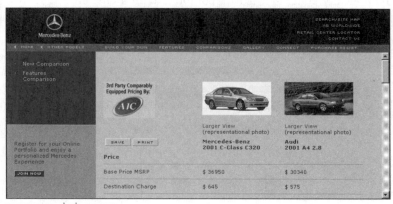

The competitive comparison on Mercedes-Benz's site is based on information provided by the Automotive Information Center (AIC), which "collects and maintains data independently of Mercedes-Benz."

www.mercedesbenz.com

Fixed Versus Dynamic Comparisons

One of the choices you have to make when implementing comparisons is whether you are going to provide fixed or dynamic ones. *Fixed comparisons* are static pages where you've preselected the items to be compared in a table. *Dynamic comparisons* enable users to select which products to compare and require much more development effort to implement.

Fixed comparisons are relatively easy to implement, but they're also easy for your users to use. These types of comparisons are best used when there is an obvious, small set of products or services to compare.

Dynamic comparisons provide your users with the capability to compare any products or services that they're interested in, but it also requires that you have a database of product and service attributes to use. Dynamic comparisons can also be a bit more difficult for your users to use than a static matrix.

The Active Buyer's Guide web site provides a fairly robust comparison tool that enables users to compare items based on their preferences. For example, users shopping for an MP3 player can select which attributes (such as price, amount of memory, and so on) are important to them and then select the MP3 players that they want to compare against these attributes. The result is a dynamically generated matrix complete with a customized score for each MP3 player based on the user's preferences.

The Active Buyer's Guide comparison tool enables users to rate and compare products based on the attributes that are important to them.

www.activebuyersguide.com

Help Users Do the Math

Overview

Help your users do the number crunching for making financial decisions, determining order quantities, or getting an estimate.

Retail

Professional

Computers by their very nature are good at math; many people aren't. Good arithmetic skills shouldn't be a prerequisite for users to do business with you. To help take the struggle out of their computations, you can provide users with calculators to help them figure out the math.

Financial Decisions

Financial

This is the most common and obvious use of calculators. Tools such as "How much home can I afford?" or "How much are my payments going to be for this loan?" have become mainstays of financial web sites. Sites like Citibank's myciti even have entire sections dedicated to calculators. These calculators are necessary because users can't go forward until these calculations have been done.

www.myciti.com

Citibank's web site has a whole section dedicated to calculators.

Ordering Quantities

Another use for calculators is for ordering quantities of goods. The Meals for You site enables you to create a shopping list based on recipes you have selected. What's neat about the shopping list is that it can dynamically calculate how much of each ingredient you need based on how many servings you want to make.

The quantities for the shopping list at the Meals for You site are calculated based on the number of servings you specify on the right.

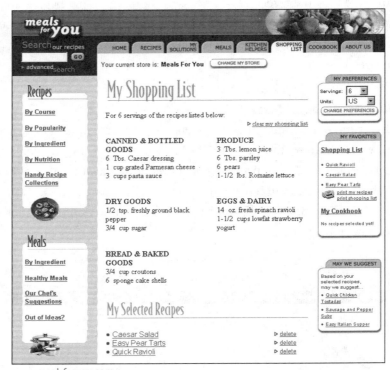

www.mealsforyou.com

Getting an Estimate

This last situation is for service providers who base their work on providing quotes. Online estimating tools provide a quick way for users to get a rough idea of the cost of their service requirements. Extima provides an online estimate for web design and hosting services based on the size and complexity of your proposed site.

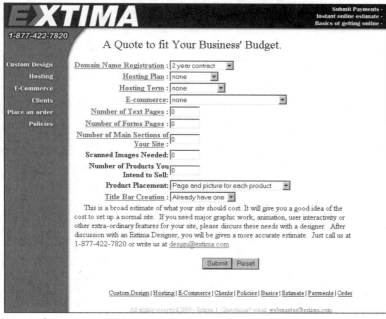

Extima's web site provides an online estimating tool so that users can know what to expect in terms of costs. One helpful aspect of this form is that the input parameters are linked to explanations of how to fill them out.

www.extima.com

The advantage of this tool is that it provides Extima's users with a better idea of costs, and it helps prequalify customers that are comfortable with the estimated costs. Compare this with another design and hosting company that doesn't provide any online estimate and that requires the customer to call in. For some customers, the path of least resistance is to go with the vendor from whom you have an estimate versus one that you don't. The risk with an online estimator, however, is that you must make your calculations reasonably accurate because your prospects will hold you accountable to the numbers.

Include a Demo Reel

Retail

Online

Financial

> **Overview**
>
> A good demonstration gives users a real feel for how your product or service will work for them—and it just might make your sale.

Demos are important to show off how something works and are an influential method of persuading users to buy. Done properly, demos can show off your online service or product and convince users that they need it.

Web Application Demos

Web application demos provide users with a glimpse of the interface they will be using for an online service. These demos are like movie trailers in that they should highlight the key points of the service and get users excited about it. What surprises me, however, is how often web-based services expect users to sign up without even seeing a screen shot of what they will be using. If you are providing an online service, a web application demo is a must-have.

You can provide the following three types of web application demos:

- **Slide show.** In a slide show demo, users navigate through selected screen shots to see how the interface works. The screen shots are usually presented with text overlays that highlight various functions and tasks. Slide shows can be taken a step further by having animated screen shots that show how users can interact with the application.

- **Interactive.** An interactive demo enables the user to actually try out the interface. Users are given access to a pseudo-functioning application that mimics the real application's behavior but doesn't actually do anything.

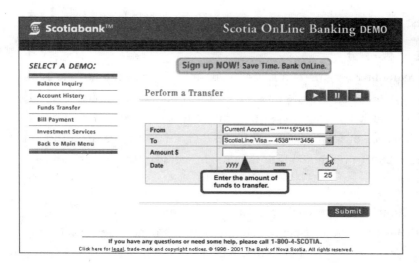

Scotiabank's demos enable users to watch an animation of the company's online banking in use, or users can try out selected functions themselves.

www.scotiabank.com

- **Guest account.** A guest account isn't really a demo, but it does fulfill the same objective of giving users a preview of your application. Users are provided with the option to log in as a guest and are given partial access to the site's functionality (or they might have full access for a limited period of time). Guest accounts help users to feel more committed to using the site, and they also entice users into wanting full access.

Some best practices for designing web application demos are as follows:

Users Need Control

Demos are about giving users a sense of control that they can use the application they are seeing. In the same way, users should have explicit control over the pace at which they view the demo. Allow them to go forward, backward, pause, or to any step within the demo. Don't force them through a 10-minute linear presentation, or they might feel like they are at a time-share presentation.

Your navigation controls should be in the exact same place on every page so that it's faster for your users to click through the demo. It's especially important for your Next button to be in the same physical location so that your users don't even have to move their mouse. Furthermore, the navigation controls should be in close proximity to one another. (For example, the Previous and Next buttons should be next to one another rather than on opposite sides of the page.) This minimizes mouse movements and speeds up navigation.

Provide an Autopilot Mode

This is an option that enables the user to sit back and just watch the demo as it goes through the steps. It's like demo TV, but you still need to provide navigation controls to allow users to pause, skip, or stop sections as they please.

Incorporate Realistic Data

The best demos are realistic ones. If you are developing a static slide-show demo, use screen shots that have realistic data input in the fields. One method is to create a fictional character and use this person's fictional information to provide continuity in the demo's content.

Show Detailed Interaction

It's also important to show the web site in its actual use. Users want to see fields being filled in, drop-down options being exposed, and buttons being pushed. If you leave these out, users will have questions as to how the application really works.

Make Sure Users Know That It's Only a Demo

I've observed some usability tests in which the users went back to the demo and thought it was the actual application! The screen shots were an exact scale to the actual application, so users got confused and started to try to click on fields and enter data. One way to get around this is to crop your screen images so that users know they are looking at screen shots. Another option is to layer animation over the screen shots so that users know they are watching a demo.

Include a Clear Call to Action

The point of your demo is to get users to sign up, so make sure you have a clear call to action integrated into every page of the demo. If your demo is appearing in a pop-up window, don't just link users to close the window. Have a separate and prominent link to a call to action that will automatically close the demo window and link the user to the action page.

Product Demos

Product demos are used to demonstrate physical products (such as furniture and toys). Two uses of demos that I've seen are relevant for physical products:

- **Assembly demo.** An assembly demo shows how a product is put together. These demos are useful for assemble-it-yourself products to help users feel confident that they can assemble the product on their own. These demos also help by providing customer service to guide your users through the assembly process.

- **Functionality demo.** A functionality demo shows how a product works. This is particularly useful for interactive products such as toys, and it explains functionality in ways that words cannot properly convey.

The MUJI ONLINE site provides animations that show how to assemble their products.

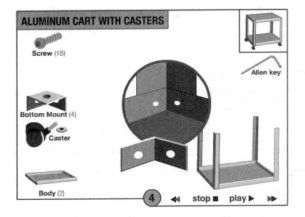

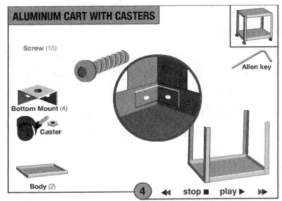

www.mujionline.com

The Fisher-Price site features toy demos that help users determine whether a toy will be appropriate for their child. This Pull-Up Ball Blast demo helps the user virtually play with the toy to see how it works.

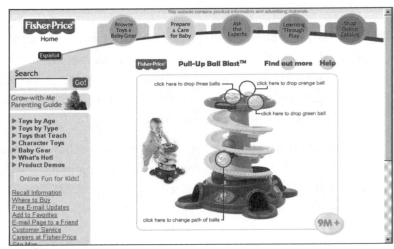

www.fisherprice.com

Design It Yourself

Overview

Allowing users to design their own solutions helps them feel more ownership of the product or service.

Retail

On your web site, you should provide evaluators with tools to help them design their own solutions. The more involved they get, the more ownership they feel. I once had a conversation with John Long, who was president of a new media company called Quadravision Communications. He told me this story about how a user designed his own solution and ended up buying it.

Online

Financial

Travel

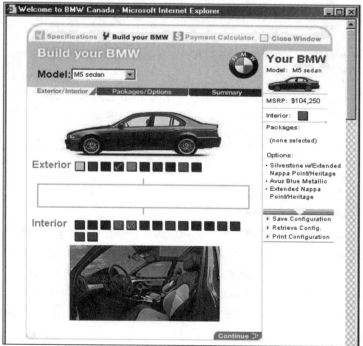

Tools like Build your BMW can help users to take ownership of products.

www.bmw.ca

This customer went to the BMW Canada web site and used the Build your BMW feature. Although this is a common feature found on car sites today, it was a pretty innovative feature at the time, given that it was 1996 and the web was just starting. What happened was that this customer virtually built the entire specifications for the BMW he wanted, printed it out, went down to the dealership, showed them his print out, and told them, "This is my car. Give this car to me." Even at this early stage, users were taking ownership of their actions on the Internet. For this customer, the fact that he designed the car created a psychological deposit where he felt like he had already bought the car in his mind.

Allowing users to design their own solution doesn't apply to every site, but here are some situations and key points for where it is useful:

Situation	Sample Products and Services	Key Points
Products with many customization options	■ Cars ■ Computers	Provide guidance for choosing between options (such as benefits, difference in price, and so on)
Personalized design	■ Photo framing ■ Furniture	Provide a preview of how the finished product will look
Itinerary	■ Conferences ■ Travel	Help users plan their activities according to a timeline

The next sections explain some tips for allowing users to design their own solutions.

Explain Design Options

Your customers don't know as much about your products or services as you do—nor should they be expected to. When you ask users to choose between design options, you should include some explanations to help them decide. Text explaining items such as "How much RAM do I need?" or "Do I need all-wheel drive?" is necessary for users to feel confident about their choices.

The Hewlett-Packard shopping site provides users with more information about their options to help them make an informed choice. Clicking on the "More info" link pops up an information window, such as the one below.

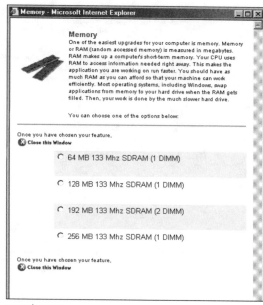

Saving It for Later

You can give users the option to save their design and retrieve it at a later visit. This can be done automatically by using a browser cookie that creates a small text file that remembers and retrieves users' designs whenever they revisit the site. Another alternative is to ask users to register and set up a user ID and password. If you go with the latter option, I would suggest that the user ID be the user's email address (it's unique and easy to remember) and that you ask for no additional information (although you might choose to ask whether the user wants to receive email updates about the designed product). Saving a custom design for later enables your users to avoid the frustration of reentering their design information—and it also gives them a reason to come back.

The Saab site lets you save and even name your car.

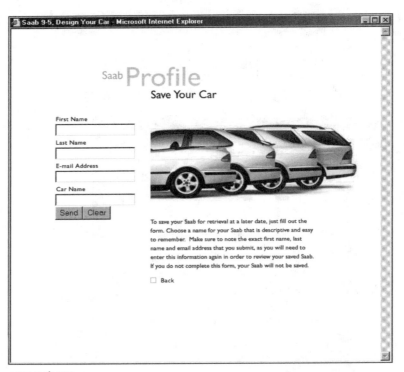

www.saab.com

Forward the Design to Someone Else

In general, products that require more customization tend to be higher ticket items. With this in mind, there's a good chance that more than one decision-maker is involved. The capability to send someone a design via email is an important one for three reasons:

1. It helps facilitate feedback between multiple decision-makers and furthers the decision process.

2. It increases the sense of psychological deposit because the user is publicly stating, "This is my design" and is sharing it with others. It's commitment and consistency in action.

3. It enables users to send the information to themselves if they happen not to be at their primary computer.

Keeping a Souvenir

One function I don't see too often is the capability for the user to save something from his or her design. It's kind of like going to a cooking class and not being allowed to take any samples home. If you give some sort of takeaway, users will feel an even greater sense of ownership.

I've often seen people change their computer's desktop wallpaper to be an image of a car that they plan to buy. These are users who are fairly committed to saying that this is their car. The only problem with these images, however, is that they might not be the exact model or color that the user wants to buy. So why not take the build-a-car concept a step further and offer users the capability to download wallpaper of the exact car they've designed? Just think how committed these users would be!

Provide a Natural Progression to the Ordering Process

This is an important point: After users have designed something, they should be able to order it right away. They've entered all the specifications, so why not lead them directly to the call to action?

Garden.com lets users plan
their garden, and then prefills
their order forms with the
elements they've laid out.

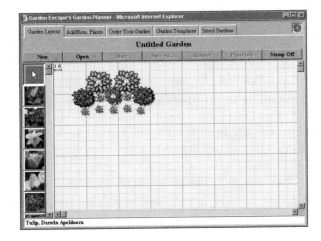

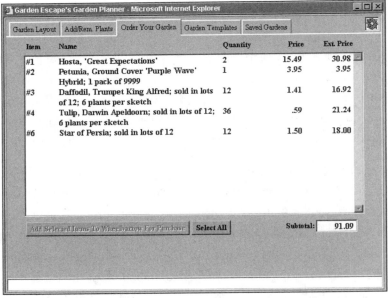

www.garden.com

Selling Your Company

> **Overview**
>
> On the Internet, you need to establish your company's credibility so that users can feel confident in doing business with you.

Retail

Professional

Online

Financial

Travel

Marketplace

When evaluators are on your web site, they need to decide not only "What should I buy?" but also "Whom should I buy from?" This is where you don't just sell your product or service; you need to sell your company. Selling your company is not just about providing your background. It's also about convincing users that you have a site where they can feel safe and secure making transactions. You need to help users trust you.

Online trust is an elusive quality, and as is in real life, you need to work hard to earn it. In the wake of the dot-com disasters, the cautiousness of users doing business on the Internet has only increased. Eliciting trust from your users is done by doing many things right, but it can be easily compromised by doing only one or two things wrong.

Provide Assurances Every Step of the Way

You need to go out of your way to give users the confidence to transact with your site. These reassurances need to be woven throughout your site. Barnes & Noble's site < **www.bn.com** > features a link to the company's "Safe Shopping Guarantee" from the main navigation bar. This guarantee reassures users that they are protected against fraud.

Amazon.com provides reassurance around its "Add to Shopping Cart" button. Users are told that they can take things out of their cart if they change their minds. Some users hesitate to click on a buy button because they fear that a transaction might go through immediately and be irrevocable. Providing reassurances like this helps give users the confidence to click to the next step.

Amazon's "Add to Shopping Cart" button puts users at ease that their transaction will not go through immediately.

www.amazon.com

Explain Your Security

Security is one of the most important concerns for users when performing online transactions, so I'm often surprised when I go to a site and find no explanation of security measures put in place to protect my information. You shouldn't expect your users to understand how security technology works nor should you rely on other sites to do the explaining for you. If you don't explain your security technology, you can't expect users to feel safe and secure in doing business with you.

I like the way that the JustWrite web site in Australia explains its security. The site provides a plain English explanation of how its security works. For example, it explains that all information on the order form is encrypted, which is further explained as "changed into meaningless data that cannot be read by anyone without the encryption key." This type of explanation is useful, accessible, and understandable by JustWrite's users, and it can help them overcome any security concerns.

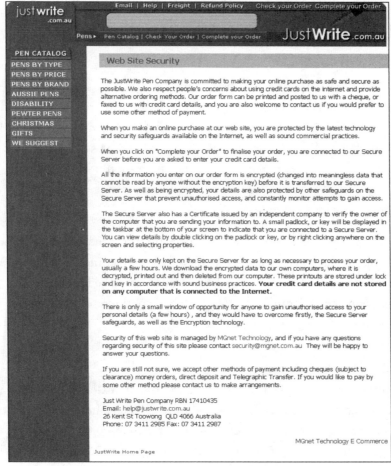

JustWrite's security explanation is simple enough to be understood.

www.justwrite.com.au

Explain Your Privacy Policy

Make sure you have a privacy policy on your site that explains what you do with information collected and how you safeguard it. Don't hide behind legalese; this will only distance your users and give them another reason to distrust you. Make your privacy policy simple and to the point so that users will believe and trust you.

You should also note that many nontechnical users don't distinguish between the concepts of privacy and security. Thus, it's important to provide privacy and security information on the same page or at the very least visibly cross-link them.

Establish Your Company's Credibility

Unless your company is a household brand with nationwide reach, you'll probably have to dedicate a part of your site to establishing your company's credibility. Given the ease with which new web sites can be set up, users will question how real the company behind the site is. You need to tell your users about yourself through information such as your company's history or your management team's experience.

List your investors, partners, and clients—especially if they have brand names that you can leverage. List your address and contact information so that users get a sense that you are a real company. Users need to know that your business is on solid footing and that they can continue to do business and receive support from you in the future.

Use Third-Party Validation

Another helpful way to establish credibility is to promote external agencies that have reviewed or audited your web site for its privacy and security policies. Displaying a recognizable logo from organizations such as TRUSTe can help boost your users' confidence. For these logos to be effective, however, the prerequisite is that your users must recognize them as credible organizations. Having a seal of approval isn't necessarily going to win your users over, but it doesn't hurt to have one.

www.expedia.com

Sites like Expedia prominently feature logos from third parties who have reviewed and approved of their privacy policies.

Don't Make Obvious Mistakes

Some of the easiest ways to undermine your credibility are to have spelling mistakes, broken links, and page layouts with broken HTML. Why? Because it gives the impression that your company is disorganized and sloppy. The remedy is simple: Check and double-check your site for mistakes so that your users won't have any doubts that you are the best site for them to transact with.

4

Transactors

Of all the groups of visitors you'll deal with—

browsers, evaluators, transactors, and customers—

transactors will be your favorite. These are the users

who have decided they want to buy your wares,

apply for your products, or use your services.

Transactors are fickle, however. At one moment, they

want to give you their business; at the next, they can

be scared off and leave your site.

This chapter will help you understand transactors, learn how you can best allay their fears, and motivate them to act. You'll learn how to remove the obstacles that might keep transactors from doing business with you, and you'll discover ways to engage them and keep them interested in what you have to offer.

To visualize a transactor, think of someone who is navigating through an obstacle course. With transactors, the emphasis should be on removing obstacles between them and their goal because they will take the easiest perceived path to reaching it. Completing a transaction is about removing annoyances, minimizing effort, and providing the right information at the right time.

I want to give you my business, so don't get in my way.

He is determined to complete the transaction, but wants safe and fast service.

He has a checkbook, credit card, and cash and wants different transaction options.

All transactors are not the same, however, and the tasks that your potential customers might want to accomplish can be quite different. There are two primary tasks that transactors might want to accomplish:

1. **Purchasing.** These transactors have decided what they want, and now they want to transact.

I've decided what to do; now let me take the next step.

2. **Continuing.** These transactors are coming back to your site for a second, third, or fourteenth time to finally make their transaction. They might have gone away to do some comparison surfing, offline research, or consultations with friends, but now they've decided to come back to give you their business.

I've come back to this site to finalize my purchase.

Provide the Shortest Path to Transact

Overview

Make your transactions quick—quick to get to and quick to complete.

Retail

Professional

Online

Financial

Travel

Marketplace

Web site users don't necessarily do all their shopping in one visit. They might go to your site, mull things over for a day or two, and then come back. Alternatively, they might have seen a product in a magazine or newspaper and decided to go to your site to find it and buy it. In any case, it's important to enable these users to transact with as few clicks as possible. This section focuses on ways you can help your users get to and complete their transactions as quickly as possible.

Make Your Call to Action Readily Available

Your call-to-action area is the area on your web site where you ask users to transact. This is the buy, apply, or contact button that you want your users to click. To capitalize when your users are ready to transact, you need to make your call to action readily available.

It All Starts at Home

For some sites, it makes sense to enable your users to begin transacting right from the home page. For a financial services site, this might mean providing access to account information or loan-application forms up front. For an online service, this translates to having your sign-up form linked from your home page. This is not about being presumptuous that your users will want to transact right away; it is about allowing predecided users to transact without having to dig through your site.

Chase's web site provides a call-to-action area on its home page that provides immediate access for transactors to apply for its banking products.

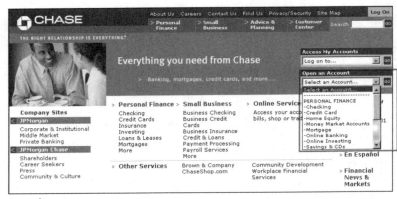

www.chase.com

List and Buy

To get to an individual product (or service) on your web site, your users will probably have to navigate through what can be referred to as *product-listing pages*. These include any pages that contain a list of products for users to gain access to. Examples of product-listing pages include your home page if it has featured items, main section and subsection pages that contain a category of products or services, and site search results when product or service matches are displayed for a user's search inquiry.

When it comes to these product-listing pages, however, don't shy away from providing a direct link for users to transact on the listed items. Don't make your users wait until they get to the individual product or service page to be able to transact. Keep in mind that you don't know whether these users are on their first visit or their eighth. It might be that these users know what they want and just want to get into the site, buy what they want, and get out.

Whether on its main section pages or its search results, Wal-Mart's product-listings pages enable users to buy (via the "Add to Cart" button) without having to go to the individual product page.

www.walmart.com

Being Available Means Being Visible

If users can't see something on your web site, it isn't there. As users scan more and more web sites, they start to develop expectations as to what certain elements (such as a buy button) should look like and where they should be located. Making your call to action available means making sure it's visible to your users. Here are some quick do's and don'ts for making your calls to action seen:

- **Don't hide them only at the very top of your pages.** If your site has only one main call to action (such as contacting you or signing up to be a member), don't just hide it in your top navigation bar. Some sites place their contact or sign-up link only at the top of each page as a means to make it available. The problem with this approach is that users might ignore the top area because that's where they expect to find banner ads, or they might only look there when they want to navigate to another section rather than to take action. The ideal place for your call-to-action area is within your main content area above the screen fold.

  ### What's a Screen Fold?

  The screen fold is an imaginary line on your web page that represents the cutoff point for what users can see without scrolling. The term is borrowed from newspapers, where the most important headlines are placed "above the fold" so that users can see them even when the newspaper is folded in the newsstand.

- **Do make your calls to action clickable.** Web users have been trained to click on two things: links and buttons. If your calls to action don't look like links or buttons, your users might be ignoring them. A definite no-no is to make your transaction links look like banner ads; in these cases, your transaction rates will definitely be low.

- **Don't be afraid to be redundant.** When it comes to your calls to action, it's okay to have redundant links leading to them. For example, if your site requires users to sign up, you might have a prominent sign-up button to the right of your main content above the screen fold, and you might also have a textual link at the end of the content at the bottom of your page so that users don't have to scroll back up to transact.

www.cafepress.com

CafePress.com enables users to set up their own virtual storefront. The main call to action is to become a member, but it's a little bit hidden. A Join button is buried in the main navigation bar, and a "Sign Up Now" link is unfortunately below the screen fold and does not look very clickable. At the very least, however, this site does have redundant links to the sign-up form.

Taking Direct Orders

As you browse through Spiegel's retail catalog, you'll not only notice the latest in spring fashions, but if you look closely at each of the product descriptions, you'll see a catalog number for each item. When users go to Spiegel's web site, they can enter this same catalog number to directly order an item. This type of directness makes it easy for your users to find exactly what they've already decided to buy.

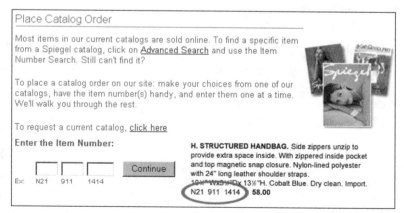

www.spiegel.com

Spiegel's web site enables users to order items directly by catalog number.

If you don't have the capability to integrate product codes with your advertisements and your web site (like the rest of us mere mortals), the next best thing is to have some visual connection between what was seen offline and what is presented at the web site. The objective is to provide an easy transition for users who have decided on a product or service; they need to be able to find and buy what they want.

On a related note, suppose you want to advertise a back-to-school sale on acid-wash jeans (in which case, it should probably be a clearance sale). On your flyer, you might want to include a graphic logo for "Back-to-School Acid-Wash Jeans Sale" throughout the advertisements. When users visit your web site, they should also see the same logo, should be able to click on it, and should see the same items that were featured in your printed flyer. Hopefully, you'll be able to sell (or get rid of) all of your acid-wash jeans.

Fork Your Transactions

When you are designing the flow of your checkout process or application form, you need to think about how you can make it as efficient as possible for your users. Take, for example, the real-life scenario of an insurance agent gathering your information for a life-insurance application form. If you smoke, he'll ask you questions 6 to 10; otherwise, he'll skip right to number 11. What the agent is doing is selectively asking some upfront questions to expedite the information-gathering process

The same logic applies to any multistep form. You need to ask your users some key "forking" questions up front and then dynamically assemble the form. For example, Kanetix is an online insurance-quoting engine. As its first question, it asks users applying for auto insurance to specify how many cars and how many drivers the quote is for. As users then click through the form, they only need to answer the minimum number of questions that are applicable to them. Instead of having a one-size-fits-all form that is longer than it needs to be, forking questions enable you to dynamically adjust the form to suit your users' needs. This increases the likelihood that they will complete the transaction.

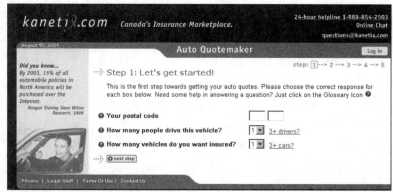

www.kanetix.com

At Kanetix, questions such as the number of drivers and vehicles are strategically placed up front to minimize the length of the overall form.

Membership Not Required

Retail

> ### Overview
>
> Don't force your users to register or create an account with you just to make a
> purchase.

So I'm happily shopping along the QVC web site, and I decide to buy the
EZ Reacher Pick-Up Tool with Saf-T-Lok so that I never have to stoop down
to pick up anything again. As I dream about my future days of a better pos-
ture, I decide to go to my shopping cart and check out when—BAM! It's the
dreaded you-must-login-or-become-a-member-first-before-you-can-shop-
with-us page. What is wrong here? I want to give the site my business, yet
it insists on me registering before I can buy.

Travel

At QVC.com, users are
required to register as a Q
Member before they can
buy items.

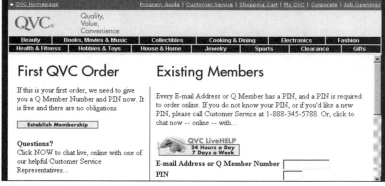

www.qvc.com

The issue with the QVC web site isn't that it asks users to become members; the problem is *when* it asks and the fact that it makes membership
mandatory before users can make a purchase. Compare this with how the
Wal-Mart web site does business, and you'll see the difference.

When I decide to check out, I am given the option to either "Begin Checkout" or "Sign In" as a registered customer. Given that this is my first time, I click to begin the checkout process. As expected, I then fill out my address, shipment, and payment details.

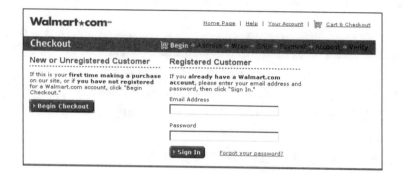

The Wal-Mart site lets users check out without registering, but it provides the option for users to create an account at the end.

www.walmart.com

When I get to the second-to-last step in the checkout process, I am given the option to submit a password to create an account. The benefit of this process is that the registration is optional, and it also explains to users that creating an account will allow them to save all the information they just entered. The advantage here is that the registration is asked for at the end (when the benefit is clearly understood) rather than at the beginning (when it seems like an unnecessary prerequisite).

Retail

Professional

Online

Financial

Travel

Marketplace

Allow Users to Transact Any Which Way They Can

Overview

Let your customers do business with you through whatever method they prefer.

A transaction is a transaction is a transaction, so however you can get one, take it. Just because users are accessing your web site, it doesn't mean they should only be able to transact online. Although you might prefer online transactions to minimize costs, if you don't display alternative transaction options, you might lose the sale altogether. Focus your efforts on converting users to becoming customers through whatever their preferred medium is, and then as they trust you more, you can focus on migrating them online.

One site that really embraces this concept is Motorola's. If you take a look at one of the site's product pages, you'll see that it provides multiple options for making a purchase: online, by telephone, or in a store. The implicit statement here is, "You can buy this product however you want to." If users are uncomfortable with purchasing online, they can call in the order. If users want the product immediately, they can locate the nearest store to pick it up. In any case, Motorola is more likely to cater to more users because of the various transaction channels presented to users.

Motorola's call-to-action area enables its users to buy through their preferred channel.

www.motorola.com

Of course, creating a site that caters to different people and the ways in which they might be most comfortable making transactions takes a solid understanding of all the different possibilities. The following sections spotlight the different ways in which your users might want to conduct business with you.

Product-Based Transactions

Let's expand on how you can allow users to buy products through a web site:

- **Buy it online.** Okay, so this one is obvious, but the section wouldn't be complete unless it was mentioned. Buying online usually takes the form of adding items to a shopping cart and then going through a checkout process that specifies delivery and payment options.

- **Shop at a store.** For those of you who have a physical presence, a simple way to get users to shop at their local store is to provide a store finder within the call-to-action area, much like Motorola has done. Simply ask your users for their zip or postal code and provide them with the addresses, phone numbers, hours, directions, and maps for the nearest locations.

  The Canadian version of the Radio Shack site takes store location one step further with an interesting function on every product page called "Find It In Store." When users click on this link, it opens a product locator window that will help them find the store locations that have the item they're looking for in stock. This is an innovative way to help users find the right location to make a purchase.

Radio Shack's Canadian site includes a product locator to help users find store locations that have a particular product in stock.

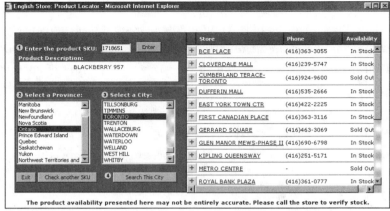

www.radioshack.ca

- **Store pickup.** A step beyond what Radio Shack does is to allow for store pickup. PartsAmerica does this by indicating which products can be picked up at a local store. When users check out, they can either have products delivered or specify a store location for pickup based on entering their zip or postal code. Think of it as e-commerce take out.

At the PartsAmerica site, users can choose from which store location to pick up their items. Will that part be for here or to go?

Option: I want to pick up from my local store:		
Store Information		**Approximate Distance**
⊙ *AKRAGEN* 1843 1/2 La Cienega Blvd, Los Angeles		4 Miles
⊙ *AKRAGEN* 6501 Laurel Canyon, North Hollywood		6 Miles
⊙ *AKRAGEN* 3899 Overland Avenue, Culver City		6 Miles
⊙ *AKRAGEN* 12420 Venice Blvd., Los Angeles		7 Miles

www.partsamerica.com

- **Call in the order.** Believe it or not, the phone is still a viable medium to receive orders. In your call-to-action area, include your phone number (with area code) and the hours (with time zone) during which you accept phone orders. To facilitate the phone order, use a unique product code (such as a catalog number and SKU) to help your users to specify the correct product.

Different Ways to Pay

Payment is the last thing you should ask your users for when they check out. When you ask for payment, you need to provide your users with as many options as possible. At the moment, the default payment method for the Internet is the credit card, but this doesn't work for everyone. Many users are still leery of credit-card fraud, and if your site is meant for teenagers, for example, they probably don't have a credit card.

Other options for payment include checks or money orders (you process the order after the check or money order arrives, but make sure your users understand that this will take longer) or alternative solutions such as Rocket Cash < www.rocketcash.com > . In the latter, you deposit money into an account from which you can then make payments.

One final option is to allow for payment on delivery. Grocery Gateway < www.grocerygateway.com > delivers your groceries to your door, and at that point you can provide your credit or debit card to pay for your order.

Show Your Payment Options

In the design of your home page, you should consider identifying which payment options you accept. It's kind of like the stickers with the MasterCard or Visa logo that are displayed at the front of a store. This helps you avoid the situation in which your users go all the way through your transaction process, only to find out that they cannot pay you.

Service-Based Transactions

If you're a service-based company or your product requires a more consultative sales approach, your main call to action is to have the customer contact you. Here are some different ways in which your users should be able to transact or request your services:

- **Send an email.** This is the simplest and most obvious way for your users to contact you. Make sure you set expectations up front in terms of your response time and clarify that any confidential information shouldn't be sent via email because it is not secure. Provide alternate email addresses for different types of service requests; this will make it easier for you to track and manage the emails.

- **Submit a contact form.** One step up from email is the contact form. This is an online form in which users can fill out their inquiry and contact information. The advantage of contact forms over email is that you can specify what information users are required to provide.

  At a basic level, you should ask users to submit a message and to specify how they want to be contacted (either via a phone number or email). If you frequently get inquiries of a certain type, such as customer complaints or sales inquiries, you might consider having additional, specialized contact forms that ask additional questions to resolve the inquiry more efficiently. The caveat, however, is to make sure you don't combine these specialized forms with your general inquiries, so that users can just send in a message by itself if they want to.

- **Make a call.** Again, the old-fashioned telephone works just fine. Don't forget to state your office hours and your area code. Your phone number should be featured on every contact page in case your users prefer not to use an online form or want an immediate response.

- **Schedule an appointment.** Many sites feature an online appointment request form. The only problem with this approach is that you might have to play email ping-pong to confirm appointment times with your customers. If you do have such an online form, make sure you ask for a phone number; it will be faster and less frustrating for you to call the customer back to negotiate a time.

A more progressive approach, however, is to display your available schedule online and then have users pick an available time slot. The Royal Touch site provides its users with the capability to view its massage therapists' schedules and to book an appointment during an open time.

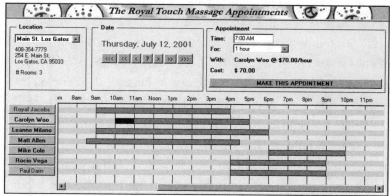

The Royal Touch's web site displays its massage therapists' schedules so that customers can schedule appointments without playing email ping-pong.

www.theroyaltouch.com

Bundle Your Offerings

Retail

> ### Overview
> Make it easy for your users to add related items to their transactions.

Once I was on a business trip where my wife asked me to purchase a particular type of scented cream at a specific store. The cream that my wife wanted was $11.50; the problem, however, was that three bottles of cream could be bought for $24.00 instead. What I originally thought would be a five-minute exercise ended up being a half-hour of internal deliberation as I debated whether I should get one item for $11.50 or three for $24.00. All of a sudden, the single bottle of cream ended up costing a lot more in my mind because the per-unit cost was significantly lower when three units were bought. This is an example of bundling in action, and it worked on me because I (or my wife, I should say) ended up with three bottles of her favorite scented cream.

Financial

Travel

When your users have decided to transact, this is a great time for you to bundle other items with their transaction. If they are going to fill out a form or go through the checkout process, why not let them make the most of the process by bundling other related offerings for their convenience? Just like the cream example, why don't you bundle items together so that your users receive a discount in exchange for purchasing multiple items? By bundling items together online, you can help your users save on two of their most important commodities: time and money. The following sections will show you different ways to bundle your offerings together.

Multiple Applications at Once

When you click on the "Apply" button at the WingspanBank site, you're lead to an application center that enables you to apply for more than one product at a time. This is a critical moment to up-sell to your users because they've already decided that they're going to transact, and now you can offer them the convenience of applying for multiple products at once. This is another type of forking question in which a minimum number of additional questions are added to the form to cover all of the products being applied for. As you promote this functionality, however, make sure you emphasize the convenience and the capability to save time by applying for multiple applications at once.

www.wingspanbank.com

Apply for as many financial products as you need all in one shot.

Would You Like Fries with That?

At a burger joint, you're never just offered a burger and a soda—you're always offered fries to go along with your meal. Web sites such as Outpost.com follow a similar idea by making it easy for users to add related items. When users are on a product page, they have two options to buy: They can buy the product by itself, or they can add related accessories to the product they are purchasing. By making these items directly accessible, they stand a higher chance of being purchased than if users were required to find and purchase the accessories on their own.

One other point to keep in mind is that this concept doesn't only apply to providing accessories for products. For example, travel sites should make it easy for users to add insurance or to upgrade their hotel room when booking vacations. The point is to make related items easily accessible so that users are more likely to add them.

Outpost.com makes it easy for users to add on related items.

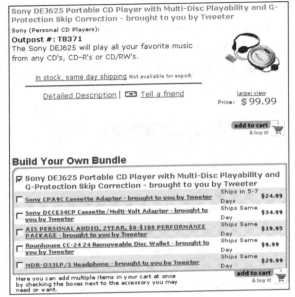

The Discount Bundle

The online equivalent of the cream example mentioned earlier can be found at Amazon.com. When users view the details for a particular book, they will see an opportunity to purchase another related book as a bundle. Similar to the cream example, the perception with this is that a better discount is offered for purchasing more items simultaneously. This technique can be fairly powerful because it leverages both a reward (getting more books) and a punishment (paying a higher separate price for each book) at the same time. The caveat in Amazon.com's case, however, is that the discount is no different than if the books were bought separately. Many users, however, will probably automatically assume that the discount is greater if they purchase the bundle and won't think twice about it.

Amazon.com's "Great Buy" bundle is difficult to resist despite not offering a better deal.

How to Gently Interrogate Your Users

> **Overview**
>
> How you ask for information is as important as what you ask for in the first place.

Retail

Professional

Online

Financial

Travel

Marketplace

Most transactions require users to provide at least some personal information, but some sites treat this process as if it were an interrogation in which information is demanded from users. Internet users often loathe providing their personal information for fear of more junk mail on how to get rich quick, lose weight, or grow their hair back. Users are skeptical about how their personal information is used, so it's important for web sites to carefully think through how and what to ask from customers to get them to complete a transaction. This section will explain how to make personal information gathering as painless as possible for your users.

The Importance of Context

If I had just met you and within the first five minutes of our conversation asked you what your salary is, whether or not you've declared bankruptcy in the last 10 years, and what your outstanding debts are, you would probably be perturbed, offended, and amazed at my intrusiveness. If, however, I were asking you the same questions as a loan officer in bank who is helping you fill out a loan-application form, you'd be quite comfortable in providing that information. The difference is the context.

An online parallel to this brings us back to the "Membership Not Required" section of this chapter, where I elaborated on how users shouldn't be required to register as a member in order to check out. iQVC.com unfortunately takes this approach when it asks new shoppers to provide their name, address, and email to register as a member before being able to check out. The problem here is that the users are being asked to provide this information in the context of becoming a member rather than in the context of checking out their shopping carts.

When it comes to asking users for personal information, you need to make sure you are only asking them questions that are relevant to the context of the task they are trying to complete. With the iQVC example, users were being thrown over to another context of membership rather than helping them with their original intent to check out their shopping carts.

Explain the Benefit

When it comes to asking users to provide information, it doesn't hurt to reinforce how doing so will benefit them. The trick is to proactively address any concerns before users hesitate and abandon the form altogether.

Take, for example, the checkout at Borders' web site. The first page asks users for the self-explanatory name and shipping address. When the site asks users for their phone numbers and email address, brief explanations are provided to explain how the information is used.

Within the Borders checkout process, users are told how providing requested information will benefit them.

Daytime Phone Number:	
	In case we need to contact you about your order.
Evening Phone Number:	
Email Address:	
	At this time, all order-related updates are provided via email. If you wish to receive these updates, please enter a valid email address above.

www.borders.com

Phone numbers are needed in case the user needs to be contacted, and email is used to keep users up-to-date on their orders. These explanations help motivate users not only to provide their information but also to do so accurately. Some users, including myself, provide fake email addresses (and I apologize to all the John Does that have received junk mail on my behalf) to bypass a form question, but if a clear benefit is explained, users are more likely to provide the appropriate information. Information needs to be treated like currency—there has to be something of value in exchange for your users to part with it.

If It's Not Required, Don't Ask for It

The Internet is a marketer's dream. It's a medium where you can interact with customers on a one-to-one basis. You can target, customize, and personalize, all in the name of building relationships. All you need is for your users to provide you with some demographics and interests and answer a few short questions for good measure.

Hold it—what's going on here? Why are we even talking about asking additional questions on a transaction form? The users' purpose is to transact, so let them. No marketing information is worth asking for if it prevents your users from becoming customers. What good is additional marketing information if it means losing customers?

Every piece of information asked for must have a meaningful purpose to support the user's current task. Every form element must earn the right to be there because every additional field is a potential barrier, a source of confusion, or an opportunity for the user to make a mistake.

The remedy is easy—if anything on your transaction form is optional, ditch it. Do it and don't look back. You'll be glad because you will have more customers.

Display Your Privacy Policy

Privacy is a top concern for many users, so it's important that it be integrated within any information-gathering form. The Nielsen-Norman Group is a usability consulting organization that also organizes conferences on the topic. For one of its upcoming conferences, the group had a simple email registration form for users to be notified of any updates:

When users are asked to provide their email address at the Nielsen-Norman Group web site, they are provided with a simple and clear (read: no legalese) privacy policy explanation.

www.nngroup.com

The strength of this design is that the privacy policy is explained in the context of the form, without requiring users to click to a separate privacy-policy page full of legal jargon (although in some cases this cannot be helped). By making this information immediate and accessible, users can have greater confidence that their information will only be used for its intended purpose.

Making Registration Seductive

Overview

Draw your users in a bit at a time and then ask for their commitment at the end.

Online

Registration can be quite a barrier, but some sites can only function properly with registered users. For example, online auction sites must have registered users to keep track of sellers with their products and buyers with their bids. Allowing anonymous sellers and buyers wouldn't make any sense. To get these users over the registration barrier, you need to engage in a bit of seductive registration.

Before you get all excited, let me explain what I mean: Seductive registration is about creating an incremental registration process in the context of the user's task. This might not sound sexy, but it certainly is a powerful idea. To see how this works, let's take a look at how two sites that allow their users to trade goods have designed their registration process.

Marketplace

SwitcHouse enables you to offer an item in exchange for something that a "seller" wants to get rid of. If the seller likes what you have to offer, you can make a trade, and the site collects a small fee. For first-time users, the process works something like this:

1. Find a product and select the option to propose an exchange.

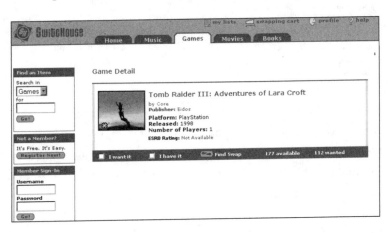

2. Sign in as a member or register to become a member.

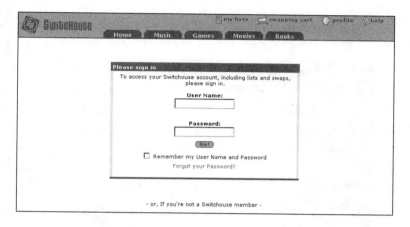

OR

www.switchouse.com

At this point, new users can decide to either register or just stop and leave the site. The problem with SwitcHouse's approach is that it comes on too strong by forcing users to register up front.

Swap.com is a similar trading site, but its registration process is more seductive in its flow:

1. Find a product and select the option to propose an exchange.

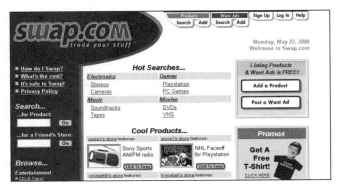

2. Sign in or continue as a guest user.

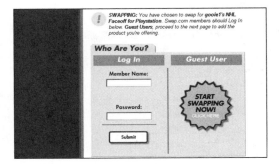

3. Propose your product to exchange.

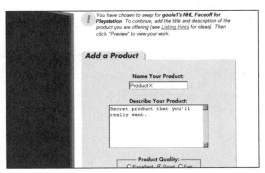

4. Confirm your offer.

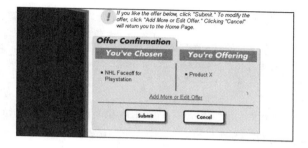

5. Register.

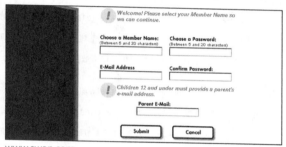

www.swap.com

The difference in Swap.com's process is that the registration happens at the end rather than the beginning. What's important is that the user is allowed to be a "Guest User" and is permitted to enter the product to be exchanged. What happens here is that the user becomes psychologically committed to making this exchange, and it's after this point that Swap.com asks the user to register. In designing your site, you need to create a path that draws users in bit by bit so that they feel committed to completing the transaction; then you can ask for registration at the end.

Taking Care of Unfinished Business

Retail

> **Overview**
>
> Sometimes when users start a transaction but just aren't ready or able to complete it, you need to provide a means for them to continue the transaction later.

Online

Financial

Travel

The online experience isn't always a continuous one. Unless you have captive users who are chained to their desks, getting on with everyday life is enough of a reason for users to stop a transaction. For complex transactions such as loan-application forms, your users might not have all the information they need to complete the form. When it comes to shopping, your users might simply be undecided. So you need to provide some means for your users to stop and then come back to pick up where they left off.

One of the challenges in allowing your users to stop and save their transactions is that you need to be able to motivate them to complete the task at a later time. Three different techniques, covered in the following sections, can help you encourage your visitors to finish their interrupted transactions.

Saving User Information

The first step is to enable your users to store the information they just entered. This can be accomplished in three ways:

- **Automatic storage.** This approach involves automatically storing users' entered information without explicitly asking them to save it. This approach is facilitated through the use of a cookie (a small text file that is saved to the user's computer that can be used to provide information back to the web site on a subsequent visit). This is most commonly used for shopping carts; items that have been placed into the cart can automatically be retrieved at the next visit. This approach, however, should not be used for any information that should remain private.

- **Explicit storage.** This is also done via a cookie, but this time users are explicitly asked if they want to store their information for the next visit. This is more appropriate for private information because the user can determine whether his or her computer is secure enough for this information to be stored (because any one user who uses that computer might be able to access this information).

At the Chase bank site, users can explicitly store their information at any point in the application process to remember it for next time. Users can also clear the information so that no one else sees it.

www.chase.com

- **Create a user ID and password.** This last option is the most cumbersome, but it also is the most secure and enables users to retrieve the stored information from any computer. This approach asks users to specify a user ID and password for accessing their entered information. Although this is more secure, it does require the user to remember yet another user ID and password combination. If you do go with this approach, make sure you send a confirmation email (see the "Providing a Reminder" section later in this chapter).

When Users Can't Decide

For retail or travel-oriented sites, users might need some time before they make a final decision. In this case, it's appropriate for you to allow these users to save or bookmark what they are interested in as an alternative to buying. Options such as "Save It For Later" or "Save It To My Wish List" provide a quick means for users to go directly back to the products they are really interested in. This type of functionality is often displayed as a secondary option under the main buy button and is usually accessible as a subsection within the shopping cart.

At the 1 Book Street site, whether you "Banish Your Belly" now by adding it to your shopping cart or later by adding it to your WishList (just under the "Add To Cart" button) is up to you.

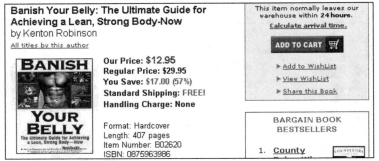

www.1bookstreet.com

Providing a Reminder

Now that your users have stored this information, you need to remind them to complete their transaction. There are two ways to provide reminders:

- **Remind them when you greet them.** When users add something to Amazon.com's shopping cart, the next time they return to the site, there's a summary of how many items are in the cart right on the home page. This method is applicable for when a cookie is used to store the user's information.

When users go back to Amazon.com's home page, they are immediately reminded that they have items in their shopping cart.

www.amazon.com

- **Send a confirmation email.** This is only applicable when you've asked your users to register and provide their email address. After your users register, you should send them a confirmation email that their information has been stored. This email can then act as a reminder for them to complete the transaction and should include a link back to the login page to access their stored information. To motivate your users to follow up, however, you might want to set and communicate an expiration date for when the information will be removed so that users don't take for granted that the stored information will always be available.

```
Hi Andrew Chak:

Just wanted to remind you about the Invite you started a few days ago. It hasn't
been sent, but fear not - it's been saved as a draft.

If you'd like to return to the Invite and/or send it out, just click below:
http://evite.citysearch.com/compose?eventID=IHJRQUBYKYJDVUZBRDIE&li=ac

This is the only reminder you'll receive for this draft - just wanted to make sure
you were aware.
If you need any help with your Invite, email us at support@evite.citysearch.com.


Your pals,

The Evite Support Team
support@evite.citysearch.com
```
www.evite.com

Reminders aren't just for unfinished application forms. Evite's site sends users an email reminder about any electronic invitations they have created but haven't finished or sent.

5

Customers

So you've turned your visitors into customers—congratulations!

The trek from browser to customer is a long one, filled with many

decisions and challenges. You started out by capturing your visi-

tors' interest and helping them choose your product or service

over your competitors'. They've filled out all the required fields in

your forms, entered their credit card numbers, and given you

their personal information. You can enjoy that feeling of comple-

tion for a moment—the first transaction has been made. Don't

get too comfortable, however, with this first achievement. Even

though this first "buy" is significant, it's the repeat business that

will make your site a success.

Your site's visitors become customers the moment they click on that submit button. These are the users who have transacted with you—your challenge and opportunity now is to get them to click with you again. This chapter will explain how to cater to these customers so that they aren't just satisfied but become loyal, repeat customers who are enthusiastic recommenders of your web site and business.

Customers expect great service, and they look something like this:

Give me a reason to do business with you again.

She wants to receive special deals and perks.

She has a VIP pass for identification and access to special areas.

She wants to know the status of her orders.

Your customers will use your web site in three different ways:

1. **Tracking.** These users want to know the status of their transaction and what should happen next.

2. **Support.** These users have specific questions or problems about the product or service they just bought or applied for.

3. **Recognition.** These users want to be recognized for who they are and are looking for any perks for being your customer. They are looking for a reason to do business with you again.

The Online Receipt

Overview

Finalize the end of every transaction by providing an online receipt.

Retail

Professional

Online

Financial

Travel

Marketplace

In the real world, shoppers go into a store, select an item, bring it to the cash register, pay for it, and get a receipt. When they leave the store, they leave with two things: the item they bought and the receipt.

In the online world, users go to a web site, select an item, add it to their shopping cart, check out, and get a confirmation. When they leave the web site, however, they don't actually get the item right away; instead, all they get is some sort of confirmation. This confirmation is even more important to online users because it's the only proof they have that the transaction actually occurred, and it's the only thing they receive immediately. If the real-world receipt is a proof of purchase, the online receipt is a proof of transaction. The next sections will discuss the two primary forms of online receipts and how to use them.

The Confirmation Page

The confirmation page is the page presented to users just after they've submitted their application form or have completed the checkout process. In fact, a confirmation page should be presented after all transactions so that users know their requests have been submitted.

When it comes to confirmation pages, here's an example of what *not* to do:

A generic confirmation screen can make users unsure about their transaction.

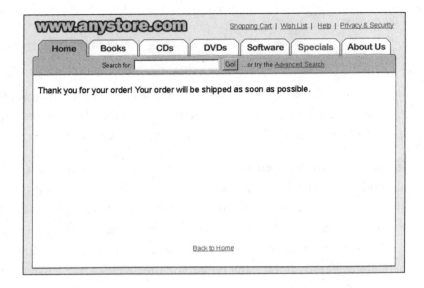

The problem with this fictional store's confirmation page is that it's too generic for users to feel that *their* specific transaction has gone through. This screen would be the equivalent of getting a printed receipt that just said "Thank you for your order" without any other details.

Before we look at what to put on your confirmation page, let's discuss the second type of online receipt: the confirmation email.

The Confirmation Email

When it comes to online receipts, a confirmation page is often not enough. Users typically expect to receive a confirmation email any time a transaction has occurred. The only exception to this is for more frequent or routine transactions such as paying a bill at an online banking site.

Confirmation emails provide users with greater reassurance because they are not as transient as confirmation web pages. After users leave a confirmation web page, it is gone, but a confirmation email can be archived. It also provides an audit trail to give users proof that their order was received.

A related type of confirmation email is the notification email. This type of email is used when there is a delayed status change in a transaction. For example, users should receive a notification email when their items ship or when their stock trade has gone through. A notification email is also important when a transaction has failed because it proactively communicates to users that a problem has occurred and that they need to resolve it.

When to Use What

The next step in terms of online receipts is to determine when and how to use each type of receipt. Depending on the type of transaction, there are different guidelines for which type of receipt should be used and what information should be presented. Here are some quick online-receipt checklists for common transactions:

Shopping Purchases

This applies to any purchase of goods or services, whether they're consumer goods (books, clothing, and so on) or travel reservations.

Confirmation Page

1. Order number (for later reference or problem resolution)

2. Order summary, including shipping costs, applicable taxes, and the total dollar amount

3. Shipping address (if applicable)

4. Billing address (if applicable)

5. Payment method (with only the last four digits of any account or credit card number showing)

Confirmation Email

1. Same information as for confirmation page

2. Return policy

3. Links to support-related FAQs or help

4. Customer support contact information

Application Forms

This applies to users who are applying for products (such as a loan) or opening an account.

Confirmation Page

1. Reference number (for later follow-up or problem resolution)

2. A confirmation as to what was applied for

3. All of the application form information that was entered

4. A reminder to users to print out this page for their records (so that they can keep track of what was submitted)

Confirmation Email

1. Reference number

2. A confirmation as to what was applied for

3. A summary of the next steps and expected timelines

4. Links to any support-related FAQs or help

5. Customer support contact information

NOTE   The entered information is not included in the email because it is not a secure means of transmitting information.

Membership Registration

This applies to users who submit a registration form to become a member of web site or to access an online service. It always involves a user ID and password setup.

Confirmation Page

In this situation, you don't need to provide a confirmation page. Instead, you should log the user directly into the customer home page for the web site or service. The sense of completion should come via the confirmation email.

Confirmation Email

1. An overview of what users can do on the web site or via the service

2. A link to the web site and its login page

3. A link to a web page that helps users retrieve forgotten passwords

4. Customer support contact information

Contact Forms

This applies to users who submit an online contact form.

Confirmation Page

1. Confirmation that the inquiry has been received

2. A confirmation number (if you have a system for tracking inquiries)

3. The expected timeline for a response

Confirmation Email

1. Same information as for the confirmation page

2. Customer support contact information

3. What to do if the user doesn't hear anything within the expected timeframe

NOTE   The confirmation email in this case is simply an acknowledgment that the inquiry has been received and is separate from the actual response.

Making It Real

One of the main purposes behind online receipts is to make the transactions real. A clever example of this is what American Airlines presents to its users after they have completed the application form to join their AAdvantage air miles program.

American Airlines presents users with their own membership card that they can print out and take away after they've completed their registration.

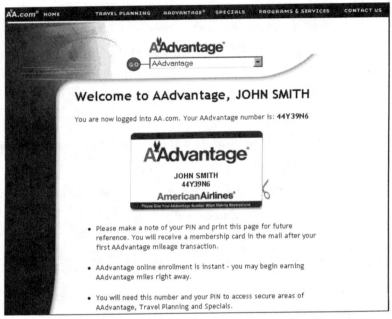

www.aa.com

The effectiveness of this confirmation screen is that users have something tangible that they can take away. By providing a combination of confirmation pages and emails, coupled with creative ideas like the preceding, you can provide your customers with a sense of completion and assurance for their transactions.

Fix-It-Yourself Transactions

> **Overview**
>
> Let your customers change their minds or fix any transactional mistakes, and they'll become that much more loyal to you.

Retail

People make mistakes, and they change their minds. If you don't let users recover from their actions, they will only change their minds about you. What kinds of decisions will your customers want to change? Here are a few examples:

Online

- Select a different product.

- Cancel their order or application form.

- Use a different credit card.

Travel

By allowing your users to change or cancel their orders, you provide them with a sense of control and begin to build a foundation of trust. It's this trust that creates loyalty that will encourage users to click back with your site again and again. The sections that follow spotlight the ways in which you can make sure your customer-recovery options live up to your users' expectations.

Provide Help

When it comes to postsale (after a purchase has been made) support, it's important that you organize a help section for your users. This is different from presales support, for which all the supporting information should be directly integrated within the product page and transaction screens (for example, directly within the signup form or shopping cart). A distinct help section is like a lifeline where your customers expect to find the answers to their transactional problems. From a recovery point of view, your help section should include the following:

- FAQs (frequently asked questions), which provide answers to the common questions that users ask

- Order information (how to track, change, or cancel an order)

- Returns and exchanges (what your policies are and what customers need to do to follow them)

KBtoys's site provides a very thorough help section that provides links to some of the most common questions that users have.

www.kbtoys.com

Order Canceling

You might cringe as you read this, but you need to let your users cancel their orders—that is, the ones that have not been shipped yet. If you don't, you're going to end up cringing later when you have to deal with accepting an item back into your inventory and risk losing a customer. As a result, you might want to give your users a grace period during which they can cancel their order for any reason. Be sure to post this on your site as a good customer-service feature.

For orders that cannot be canceled (if your orders are immediately processed or if your products are custom made), you need to explain why within your help section. Information should then be provided regarding the best way to return the order. One creative suggestion I've seen is a retailer who suggested that the user simply refuse to accept the package upon delivery. This provides an easy way to get the item back to the merchant at minimal cost to the user.

Return and Exchange Policies

Suppose one of your dependable repeat customers wants to return a pair of plaid shorts that he purchased online. How are you going to graciously accept his return (although I can't understand how you can be gracious about anything plaid) and make sure you keep his future business? By clearly stating your return and exchange policy, you can help set and steer your customers' expectations. Your return and exchange policies should include the following:

- **Deadlines.** Tell your customers how long they have to return or exchange items. Identify any products that have a different time period for accepting returns or exchanges or if you have different deadlines during holidays.

- **Exceptions.** List any products for which you will not accept any returns or exchanges (such as custom-made goods). This information should also be available directly on the product pages.

- **Conditions for accepting returns.** Explain the condition that the merchandise must be in for a return or exchange to be accepted. (For example, CDs must still be in their original shrink-wrap.)

- **The process.** List the steps that the customer must take to ensure a quick return or exchange. Provide detailed instructions for how to package and ship the item back so that it's easier for you to receive it and process the return. (In fact, these instructions—along with a preprinted return-shipping label—should be included with the order in the first place.) An expected timeline for resolution (that is, how long it will take for a refund) should also be communicated.

- **Additional charges.** Manage your users' expectations ahead of time by clearly stating any additional charges that users have to pay such as shipping charges and restocking fees.

Ashford is a luxury items site that provides a clear, detailed description of its returns process.

Here is the simple process for returning an item to Ashford:

1. Contact our customer care team by either calling 1-888-922-9039 or e-mailing us at returns@ashford.com to obtain a Return Merchandise Authorization (RMA) number. The RMA number must be written on your original invoice and on the pre-printed return-shipping label, which will be included with your order for your convenience.

2. Repack the product in its original packaging materials. In the case of diamonds, enclose the original copy of the matching or identifying certificates.

3. If the product you're returning included a special offer or a "gift with purchase," return that item as well, or you may choose to have the cost of that item subtracted from your refund.

4. Affix the enclosed, pre-printed return-shipping label to the package, and do not include any other markings or text on the package. Ship your return prepaid and insured for the full purchase price by a trackable carrier such as United States Postal Service registered mail, United Postal Service, or Federal Express to the address listed on the pre-printed label.

If you are returning a product because it was defective or we shipped you an item that you did not order, Ashford will pay the return-shipping costs. In no event will Ashford be responsible for return-shipping losses.

www.ashford.com

Allowing for Human Contact

Some web sites feel like unmanned deep-space probes that run remotely from top-secret military bases—you know there are people running the site; it's just that you can't find how to contact them. One of the false assumptions that designers often make is that if users are choosing to use a web site, they probably want to be serviced via the web. Coupled with a motivation to reduce customer inquiries, some web sites have chosen to hide their contact information as if it were part of a scavenger hunt. The shortcoming with this approach is that sometimes direct human contact is the best way to interact with a customer. In fact, most users would probably prefer to resolve their problems with a real live person to close the issue quickly. Here's a quick look at a couple of human contact options:

- **Online chat.** Online chat puts your users in direct contact with your customer service representatives through short text messages that are exchanged in real time. Online chat is best used for quick questions that do not require extended responses. Chat makes it easy for users to ask quick questions that they might not have bothered with if they had to compose an email. Despite the additional questions, chat does help lower the number of emails, and it provides customers with more responsive service that might be critical to help users through a transaction.

- **Phone number.** Your phone number (preferably toll-free) should be prominently displayed throughout your site. Although its prominence might generate more calls, it will also provide you with an opportunity to salvage any dissatisfied customers who otherwise might not call and might just choose to leave your web site.

Tracking Transactions

Retail

Professional

Online

Financial

Travel

Marketplace

> ### Overview
> Always provide the capability for users to track the status of their transactions before they resort to tracking you down.

Provided that you've given a transaction number to your customers, the next logical step is to enable them to track their orders. Anything that is ordered online should be tracked online—whether it is a product, a service request, or an application. For users, an online-tracking system is like having a living digital receipt that reassures them that their order is being taken care of.

Tracking Shipments

The most common form of order tracking is to enable users to track their order shipments. After an order has been submitted, a notification email with a shipment tracking number should be sent when the order has shipped. What some sites do is provide a shipment status query that links users directly to the shipping company's tracking database to find the shipment's status.

Belkin's tracking page provides a convenient way for users to track their shipment status regardless of the shipment company used.

www.belkin.com

Tracking Applications

A variation of order tracking is to track the status of an application form. Take, for example, what Fieldstone Mortgage Company does by enabling its loan applicants to track the status of their mortgage application:

Welcome, Amber! Thank you for choosing Fieldstone Mortgage Company for your borrowing needs! Your online application was received on SEPT-3-99. We received your completed loan package on SEPT-13-99. Your loan is now in the Underwriting Stage. If you have any questions during the loan process please feel free to call [redacted], your dedicated loan consultant at 800-959-8084.

Setup	Your application was received on	SEPT-3-99
	Your loan package has been mailed to you.	
Processing	Your loan documents were received on	SEPT-10-99
	Your appraisal was ordered on	SEPT-11-99
	Your appraisal was received on	SEPT-13-99
	Your loan was locked on	
Underwriting	Your loan package has been sent to underwriting	SEPT-13-99
	A decision was received from underwriting on	
Documents	Your loan documents were ordered on	
Title/Closing	Your loan documents were sent to the closing agent and are available for signing.	
	Your loan has funded.	
	Your loan is now closed and has been recorded.	

Loan Details | Document Tracking | Appraisal | Closing Cost Details | Customer Service

www.fieldstonemortgage.com

The "statusTRACK" feature at the Fieldstone Mortgage Company site enables users to see how their loan application is moving through the process.

The strength of Fieldstone's loan-status tracker is that it exposes users to the next steps and manages their expectations in terms of the length of time required to process their application. This type of online status also provides a feeling of comfort because it makes the users feel like they are being taken care of. For Fieldstone's customers, this is especially important because mortgages have such a significant impact on people's lives.

Here are some general guidelines to follow for order tracking:

- **Set expectations.** Clearly explain how up-to-date the order information is and set expectations if the information is updated any less frequently than real time (for example, once a day).

- **Use email to keep people up-to-date.** A notification email should be sent with each status change in the order. Be very careful with the wording of your notification emails to make sure it is accurate. I once received an email for an e-commerce order that stated my order had left the warehouse and was on its way, only to receive a follow-up email stating that the item was out of stock!

- **Provide offline contact information.** Don't be afraid to include your phone number to provide support—if you hide it, your customers will be even more irate with you when they call.

- **Anticipate further courses of action.** In some instances, such as with application forms, it's helpful to provide users with more information that supports further courses of action. At the University of South Florida's graduate admissions web site, the "Tracking an Application" page explains all of the steps of the application process and provides more information on likely next steps (such as appealing a denial of admission).

If users don't get accepted to a University of South Florida graduate program, they will at least know where they can appeal the decision.

> **Step Four: The Admissions Decision**
> When the program has made an admissions decision regarding an application, that decision is submitted to the Office of Graduate Admissions for review and processing. Some programs also send a letter to the applicant informing him/her of the recommendation for admission that has been sent to the Office of Graduate Admissions; however, **an applicant should not consider any admissions decision as official until receiving an official correspondence from the Office of Graduate Admissions.** Applicants may check on the status of their applications *after* a decision has been processed by going to **http://sonic2.grad.usf.edu/App_Status/Status.asp**. Admitted applicants should also refer to **Types of Admission**; denied applicants should see **Appeals/Denial of Admission.**

www.usf.edu

Transaction History

A transaction history provides a record of all orders—both pending and fulfilled. Because this is transactional data, an explicit user login (discussed in the next section) should be required. The details behind each transaction should include what was ordered, the date, shipping and billing information, the payment method, and the order's status. If the order has been shipped, the shipping company's tracking number should be referenced. If the order is cancelable, the option to cancel should be provided as per the previous section.

Identifying Your Customers

> **Overview**
>
> To service your customers, you need to provide a convenient and secure way for them to identify themselves.

Retail

Professional

Online

Financial

Travel

Marketplace

Customers expect service—they've given you their business, and they expect to be taken care of in return. As customers return to your web site, however, you need to identify them so that your site can give them personalized service. At the same time, you also need to make the identification process stringent enough to provide customers with a sense of security and exclusivity.

Identifying customers is about providing them with access—access to exclusive promotions, to previously entered information or transactions, and to more personalized service. Depending on what your customers intend to do, you will need to employ different customer-identification techniques based on maintaining that balance between convenience and security. The sections that follow introduce you to these customer-identification methods in more detail.

"C" Is for Cookies

Cookies are the easiest and simplest way for users to be identified because your customers don't need to do anything. Cookies are small text files stored by your users' web browsers on their computers. When they go back to your web site, the cookie is read, and your users can be automatically identified. If you were to compare this type of security to gaining entry to a building, it would be like having someone from inside the building recognize you as you approach and automatically open the door for you.

Which Method Is Best? All of the Above

Each of the customer-identification methods discussed has perks and problems. The following table details the pros and cons of each of the identification approaches:

Cookies	Gated Login	Just-in-Time Login
Pros	**Pros**	**Pros**
The easiest and most convenient means for users to be identified	Greatest perception of security	Seamless integration between content and transactional areas— great for cross-selling
No passwords to forget		
Good for retrieving preference settings and nonpersonal information		
Cons	**Cons**	**Cons**
The least secure option	Creates a wall between content and transactions	The most complex option to implement
Unsuitable for publicly shared computers	Requires users to remember a user ID and password	Requires users to remember a user ID and password
Some users might disable cookies within their browsers		

The best approach is to use a combination of all these identification methods. The My Yahoo! < my.yahoo.com > personalized portal provides a good example of how to combine all three:

The Anonymous User

Users who aren't logged in require explicit entry of their user ID and password. They also have the option of being automatically remembered (via a cookie) for their next visit.

Automatic Login

This is the customized Yahoo! home page that displays if users have chosen to be automatically remembered for login. Otherwise, users will be prompted for their user ID and password.

Just-in-Time Login

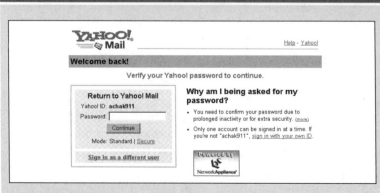

my.yahoo.com

When users are accessing personal or transactional areas of Yahoo!, they are asked to identify themselves by providing a password again.

Getting to Know Your Customers

Retail

Professional

Online

Financial

Travel

Marketplace

> **Overview**
> To personalize your customers' experiences, you need to know them. The best way to know them is to take note of what they actually do.

You've probably heard that for your business to succeed, you need to know your customers. By knowing your customers on a one-to-one basis, you can individually cater to their needs to facilitate the next transaction.

How Not to Profile

Oftentimes, the approach for getting to know customers is getting to know their demographics. How old are they? Where do they live? Do they have 2.5 kids? These demographics are usually collected by asking users to fill out a personal profile so that products and information can be targeted to them based on some rules. For example, if Gary is 25, lives on his own, and has no kids, he might fit the demographic profile of an audiophile and be targeted with home-stereo-system promotions. On the other hand, 30-year-old Genny, who lives in suburbia with a baby on the way, would receive targeted links for the latest in strollers. In either case, a static profile is collected and is referenced for targeting ongoing promotions.

The first issue with this type of profiling is that the information collected might be inaccurate. If users are filling out a profile, they might be careless in providing information because there are no apparent consequences for making a mistake (other than finding out more about strollers than they might care to).

Sometimes users are asked to fill out a profile prior to gaining further access to a web site. The problem here is that users have no motivation to provide the correct information. I've known many people who have filled out demographic profiles about themselves to get free subscriptions to computer magazines. To qualify for the subscriptions, these individuals suddenly found themselves being "promoted" to chief information officer or senior vice president of technology and being in charge of a seven-figure annual budget. In this case, the profile is a barrier that users will shy away from altogether, or they might just tell you the information you want to hear.

The second issue with a profile is that the information collected is only valid for a given period of time. When Genny says she has one baby on the way today, what about in a couple of years? What about in 10 years? The problem with collecting a static profile is that there is no motivation for users to keep it updated. Users might continue to receive promotions on diaper wipes when their offspring are in college. In this case, the users might just opt to ignore the site rather than recognize the need to update a profile to receive better-targeted promotions.

To overcome the limitations of static profiling, let's look at a couple of pro-filing techniques that provide more accurate and up-to-date information.

Contextual Profiling

This type of profiling basically targets information to users based on what they have just done or told you. Take, for example, the scenario of someone completing an online application for a loan. During this process, the user provides a lot of personal information such as age, income, address, assets, and liabilities. Once completed, the user submits the information and receives a confirmation that the application has been submitted.

The opportunity here is to introduce a related product that matches the information just entered. If the user has a high income, you might target a promotion for a Visa gold card. If the user has a lot of liabilities, you might target a debt-consolidation service. The point is not to go out of your way to profile your users; instead, you are to pick up on what they have told you through the normal course of their transaction and target promotions to them immediately.

One word of caution, however, is that contextual profiling is only for an immediate point in time. When someone buys diapers once, you can imme-diately present a related link to changing pads. That doesn't mean, however, that you should continue targeting similar products from that point on; otherwise, you might end up being more irritating than a diaper rash.

After ordering tickets for a show at the Ticketmaster Canada site, I am given many links on the right to related items. "What's Near the Venue?" contains a list of bars and restaurants that are personalized based on their proximity to the venue I've selected.

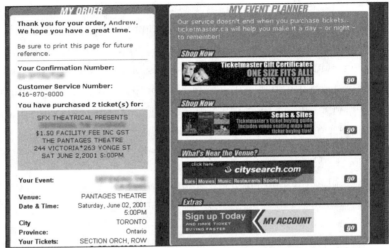

www.ticketmaster.ca

Cumulative Profiling

This approach builds a user's profile over time. A cumulative profile observes user activities and transactions and targets new items based on the accumulated data, although greater emphasis is placed on more recent actions. This type of approach can be more accurate because it relies on what users actually do over time.

The one shortcoming to this approach is that it assumes the users are performing all of their activities for themselves. At Amazon.com, you could be forever mislabeled as a green thumb if you to decide to buy a gardening book for Aunt Nelly. One way to get around this is to enable users to identify items that aren't for themselves so that the transaction doesn't get factored into the accumulated profile.

NOTE   For some suggestions on what to do with all of this profile information, see the "Set Up the Next Transaction" section later in this chapter.

Let Customers Tell You How Bad You Are

Overview

Have a plan for facilitating and collecting customer feedback to identify opportunities for improving the user experience.

Retail

Professional

Online

Financial

Travel

Marketplace

Even a customer who is a thorn in your site—complaining about load times, dead links, confusing maps, and so on—can play an important role in improving your site. Every site can be improved in some way—the trick is to listen to the problems your customers are having (as well as their likes and dislikes) and to work them into future revisions of your site. Customer feedback is particularly important because these people have gone through the process from end to end and can provide the most complete perspective on how you can improve their next transaction.

Although it might sound counterintuitive, you need to encourage your users to bring up any problems they might have. Collecting customer feedback, especially from unhappy users, is important for a couple of reasons:

- Just allowing customers to articulate their problems can improve their loyalty to you.

- Those who complain tend to care about your web site the most and are more likely to be frequent users.

So, in fact, allowing your customers to vent will help to make your most frequent users more loyal!

It's important that you actively encourage feedback; otherwise, users will do the simple thing and leave you. By encouraging customer feedback, you at least provide the opportunity for users to approach you to resolve their issues. Furthermore, if you resolve the problem, these users will like you even more.

Email

The simplest form of feedback is an email link. Anything your customers send you is a form of feedback. Depending on your resources, you might consider listing specific email addresses to which customers can direct their inquiries. The downside of multiple email addresses is that users are required to figure out to which email address they should send their comments, but the upside is that you're able to track what the recurring issues are.

A more advanced way to handle email is through an email form. These forms can be particularly helpful with problem resolution because they can help prompt customers to provide the appropriate information to solve a certain type of problem.

Sites like JC Penney's offer separate email forms for different types of inquiries. Each email form asks users to provide different pieces of information depending on the topic.

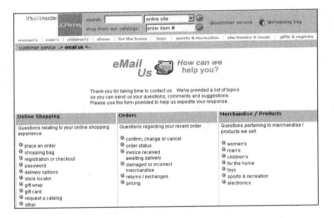

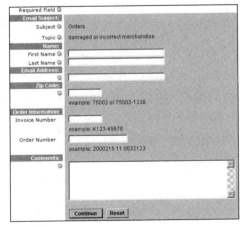

www.jcpenney.com

Surveys

Online surveys can provide a quick way for you to gather feedback on your site, but the results need to be taken with a grain of salt. The reason for this lies in the motivations that users have in completing the survey in the first place.

Users who fill out surveys to win a prize might carelessly provide any old answer just so that they qualify. If no incentive is offered, it's more likely that unhappy users will be the ones who fill out your survey and negatively influence the results. One effective and perhaps less biased means for motivating users is to give a charitable donation for every completed survey. This helps users feel good about themselves and encourages them to be more honest with their answers.

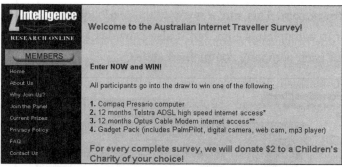

Sites like ZIntelligence positively motivate users to participate in surveys by making a donation to charity for every completed survey.

www.zintelligence.com

Another important element of surveys is the context in which they are presented. If you are collecting information about why people use the site, you should present it off of the home page. If you're collecting information about the entire experience, you should present the survey just after the user has completed a transaction. It's important for the survey to be presented at the exact right time to collect feedback when the user still has the right mindset. Don't pop up a survey as users are leaving your site; they will only become more annoyed and stand an even smaller chance of returning.

Other Sources of Feedback

If you find that you're not getting enough direct feedback from your users, you can always look to external sites to review what they are saying. Search

Send an Acknowledgment Email

Anytime a user contacts you, you're responsible for responding in a timely manner. If you cannot respond to your customers' inquiries within one hour, you should send an acknowledgment email stating that their contact has been received. The acknowledgment email should communicate the following:

- That the inquiry has been received

- That the problem is being worked on

- The expected timeframe for a formal response

Fix the Person and Then the Problem

When customers come to you with a problem, they are vulnerable and, in their own way, broken. When writing an email response, you need to fix the customer as well as the problem itself. Fixing the customer means empathizing with him and recognizing the inconvenience he's gone through. A useful tactic is to repeat the problem back to the customer in your own words.

If the problem isn't caused by your organization (for example, a customer purchased software from you that causes his computer to crash), you still need to acknowledge the problem because your customers will associate that problem with you. Even if you can't fix the problem yourself, try to refer the customer to resources that can help him.

Inform Your Users

Information is power, and sometimes you need to provide information to your users as to why the problem occurred and how they can avoid or solve it themselves the next time. If your users improperly fill out an application form, explain to them what went wrong and how they can correct it the next time to avoid delays. If they order the wrong product, link them to a resource that will help them make the right decision the next time. It's frustrating for users to have to resort to contacting you, so by providing them with information, you can make them feel much more secure and in control.

Don't Just Respond, Provide a Solution

I once bought a VIP membership at a local movie theater that gave me validated parking at a nearby parking lot. The day I bought the membership, however, I had already paid for my parking. My first question was then, "Can I get a refund for my parking today?" The dumbfounded response I received was a simple, "I don't know." I stared silently at the teenage cashier for a few moments, expecting something more like "I'll find out for you if I can," but I waited in vain. This is an example of someone who simply responded to my inquiry but didn't do anything about it. Don't just acknowledge that a problem exists; provide your customers with a solution.

Create Response Templates

As you begin to address customer problems, you should start accumulating a set of response templates for commonly occurring problems. These templates provide you with a means to address similar problems in a consistent manner. As you develop these templates, their content should be migrated toward your FAQ or help section (or even your product pages). If these problems are causing frustration for your customers, you should consider revising your site to resolve the problems.

Include Your Phone Number

Whether it is your 1-800 number or otherwise, you should provide your users with convenient access so they can phone you to facilitate a more immediate resolution. Don't hide that number!

Provide a Personal Touch

There's nothing more satisfying to customers than receiving personal attention to solve their problems. Your responses to customers shouldn't just be a mechanical cut and paste of response templates. Responses should be personalized to each customer's initial inquiry. Furthermore, whoever is responding should include her first name as well a direct-contact email address or phone number for any further resolution. This helps reassure customers that they are being individually taken care of.

Suppose a customer had emailed to you this request:

```
Dear company:

Last week, I ordered some RAM to upgrade my Compaq computer.
I bought 128MB. When I received it, I tried to install it,
but it wouldn't fit within the RAM slots on my computer. I
spent more than three hours trying to figure this out to no
avail. How do I return this to get my money back?

John Smith
```

Using the principles in this section, here's how you might respond:

Dear John:

I'm sorry to hear that you didn't receive the right RAM for your computer—I've done a few upgrades with my own computer, and I can understand how frustrating it can be.

To get a refund, please call us at 1-800-COMPANY. We'll give you a return merchandise authorization (RMA) number. Then follow these steps:

1. Write the RMA number on your invoice and the preprinted return-shipping label. (You should find this within your original shipment.) Unfortunately, we cannot accept returns without the RMA number.

2. Place the RAM back in the original package, and affix the preprinted return-shipping label on the package.

3. Send it back to us via a trackable carrier such as UPS or Federal Express.

If you still want to upgrade your computer, may I suggest that you try using the RAM Matcher on our web site? By entering the specific model number of your computer (usually found on the back of the computer), you can find and link to the exact RAM you can use to upgrade your computer. The RAM Matcher can be found at www.company.com/rammatcher.

If you need any further assistance, feel free to call or email me directly. Happy computing!

Greg Mitchells
gmitchells@company.com
1-888-COMPANY ext. 251

The customer is addressed by name.

Repeating and acknowledging the problem helps to empathize with the customer.

The customer's question is answered in a detailed manner. Given that this is probably a frequently asked question, this text should be from a response template.

Useful information empowers the user with the real solution to his problem and also prompts him to come back to the site.

A personalized closing provides a personal touch that the user will appreciate.

A specific name, email address, and phone number makes it easy for the user to ask any additional questions and makes him feel like he is being personally attended to.

Turning Customers into Sellers

Overview

Make it easy for your customers to be your most effective sales force.

Retail

Online

Financial

Travel

Marketplace

Your customers are valuable—not only are they your best candidates for generating more business, they can also be your best way to acquire new customers. Instead of spending more money on marketing, consider investing in building site functionality that will help current customers become part of your virtual sales force.

Potential customers are much more willing to purchase products or services from people or companies that they know as opposed to purchasing from a complete stranger or a site that has no relation to them. This is an old trick that many salespeople employ. If they aren't successful in selling you something, they'll ask for some referrals because they know it's an effective method of getting in the door—or Inbox—of new prospects. The next sections will discuss two ways in which you can turn your customers into sellers.

The Email Referral

The quickest and easiest way to turn your customers into sellers is to allow for email referrals. This works by enabling customers to send promotions to their friends; their friends then receive a direct link to a sign-up page that also captures who they were referred by. This method works best if the customer, as the referrer, is rewarded for doing so and if those receiving the referral also receive some sort of benefit. Amazon.com has a pretty compelling model that motivates both the sender and the receiver of the referral.

The referral process starts when a customer makes a purchase. After the transaction is concluded, the customer is given the option to "share the love" (I don't make this stuff up, I swear), which enables the customer to enter the email address of someone they know. That person will then be allowed to enjoy a discount on the same products just purchased. If the referral recipient makes a purchase, the original customer receives a discount on future Amazon.com purchases. The key here is that everyone benefits—both users get a discount, and Amazon gets a more persuasive virtual sales force.

Amazon.com's "Share the Love" program encourages me to take advantage of a special discount so that my friend Amanda can also earn a discount.

Receivers Become Members Who Become Senders

Another way to turn your current customers into sellers is by requiring recipients to become members. For example, Paypal < www.paypal.com > is a service that enables its customers to send payments to others via email. Payees will then receive an email notification telling them that there is a payment waiting for them, but the catch is that they must be members to receive any payments. When these users become members, they need only to provide a bit more information to send payments themselves.

This setup has helped Paypal grow to over 10 million registered users with an average of 18,000 accounts being added per day—with virtually no traditional sales or marketing. The catch here is that PayPal has something that users want: money that's owed to them. When it comes to your site, you need to give users a similarly compelling offer for them to consider joining.

Set Up the Next Transaction

Overview

Give users a reason to do business with you again—and make that next transaction easy.

The first time that users become your customers, they are one transaction closer to becoming profitable for your company. In fact, it takes an average of three to four transactions before a user brings any profit to you—that's all the more reason to make sure they are not one-hit wonders. Making the next transaction easier helps create customers who are more loyal, more profitable, and less price sensitive, and who provide better referrals.

Your goal is to get your users to make at least three transactions. A study by the Boston Consulting Group[1] suggested that it takes three transactions to make an impression on users:

1. **Trial purchase.** This first purchase is where your acquisition dollars pay off. Your users have taken an initial step of faith.

2. **Confirmation purchase.** This second purchase is used to verify whether the first experience was a fluke or not.

3. **Cementing purchase.** This third purchase is where the relationship begins to lead to loyalty and is where most retailers break even on customer-acquisition costs.

The sections that follow will discuss how to make sure your first-time customers become repeat customers.

---

[1] "The State of Online Retailing," a study by Boston Consulting Group, Boston, Massachusetts, July 1999.

Get Them to Transact Again

Assuming you've provided your customers with great service, you need to nudge them into becoming browsers to start the whole decision cycle over again. Here are some ways to get your users to restart that decision cycle:

- **Keep your home page fresh.** Users judge a web site by its home page in the same way that we tend to judge a magazine by its cover. It's important for the home page to always look fresh—either by rotating existing content or by providing new featured content. The objective is to always highlight something new for returning customers to pique their interest about something and turn them into browsers.

- **Send an email newsletter.** Email newsletters give you a valid reason for keeping in touch with your customers. Some guidelines for writing and sending your newsletters are as follows:

  - **Be targeted.** Allow your users to select the type of content they want or target information to users based on their profile.

  - **Provide newsletter options.** If you can, produce different newsletter sections that users can decide to subscribe to or not. Topic ideas include highlighting new items, special deals, value-added content related to what your business offers (to draw users in as browsers), and value-added content related to enhancing the products and services they've bought from you.

newsletters

☐ **What's in Store™** (sent approximately once a month)
Essential picks and top sellers from our store come to you. Learn how to live well, look better and feel great.

☑ **Great Deals** (sent approximately twice a month)
Be the first to hear about free offers, biggest savings and best deals.

☐ **GNC Newsletter** (sent approximately once a month)
Sign up and never miss a sale on vitamins, supplements or nutrition aids from our GNC Live Well Store.

☐ **Beauty Bulletin** (sent approximately once a month)
Discover the hottest picks and trends from our prestigious online beauty boutique, Beauty.com.

reminders and updates

☑ **Your List** (sent as often as you choose)
Finish your shopping in 5 minutes or less with this record of your previous purchases. Notifies you when your favorite items are on sale.

How often should we send Your List? [1 month ▾]

☐ **Headlines**
Exceptional store news and special announcements.

format preferences

Choose your e-mail format preference:
● HTML ○ Text ○ AOL

www.drugstore.com

Drugstore.com's various newsletters highlight new items, special deals, and beauty tips. One nice touch is the fact that the frequency of the newsletter is also mentioned.

- **Provide exclusive customer offers.** Using exclusivity as a tactic, provide offers made only to your customers and communicate to them how valuable they are.

- **Remind them of your site's features.** At the end of your newsletter, highlight functional features of your site that make it easier for users to transact (such as shopping lists or express application forms).

- **Provide an alternate text version.** If you're sending your newsletter only in HTML, you should include a link to an online version of it in case a user has an email client that cannot render HTML. Otherwise, just provide a text option for users when they subscribe.

- **Provide an unsubscribe option.** Last but not least, always provide an unsubscribe option; otherwise, your users will get really annoyed.

Make the Next Transaction Easier

As customers (hopefully) transact with you more and more, you should look for ways to make each transaction a little bit easier. Here are some ideas:

- **Shopping lists.** If yours is a retail site with items that are often replenished, shopping lists make a lot of sense for you. These lists provide quick access for users to reorder frequently purchased items.

Drugstore.com's "Your List" feature enables users to store their frequently purchased items and have a reminder email sent to themselves to reorder the items at a preset frequency.

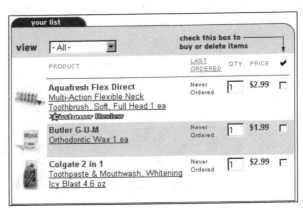

www.drugstore.com

- **Prefilled fields.** Nothing makes a form easier to fill out than if you pre-fill the fields for your users based on the information you've collected from them before. For example, if you're a financial services site, don't make your users fill out a completely blank application form every time they apply. Instead, prefill whichever fields you already have from their previous applications. This will make it a faster process for your users to apply for additional products.

- **Express transactions.** Amazon.com changed its checkout process to make it faster for repeat customers to complete their transactions. When users decide to check out, they are asked to log in and are brought to a confirmation page with their default billing, shipping, and payment options. At this point, users can either place their order or can choose to edit the transaction options. For the returning customer, this approach makes the purchase process much more efficient.

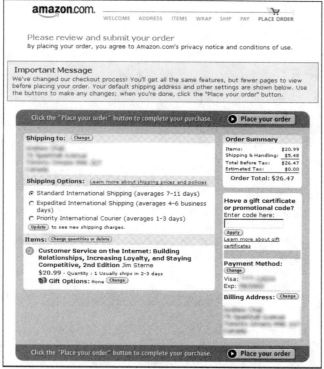

Amazon.com provides repeat customers with an express checkout process that can reduce the number of steps from five to one.

www.amazon.com

6

The Design of Everyday Pages

Now that you understand the consumer-decision

cycle and the needs of different users coming to

your site, you're ready to think about the part

that the actual pages' design plays in creating a

persuasive site.

Computer users are accustomed to seeing certain conventions on the web that help them know where to look, what to click, and how things work. For example, navigation bars are typically at the top or side of a page, links are often blue and underlined, and items need to be placed in a shopping cart to be purchased. This kind of familiarity makes browsing and buying easier because people know what to expect from sites in general and aren't required to learn how a site works each time they visit a new one.

This chapter is about designing the everyday pages that are commonly found on web sites. Designing everyday pages is about leveraging users' expectations regarding how certain types of pages work to make it easier for them to immediately understand how to use them. This is not an argument to make sites bland and just like everyone else's; it's about making sites easy to figure out so that the design doesn't get in the way of transactions. Designers shouldn't necessarily make all retail sites look like Amazon.com nor all portals like Yahoo!, but they should leverage the conventions that sites like these have started to establish.

Let's take a look at a real-world, tangible example. Each of the following doors is different—they have different layouts, colors, and styles:

   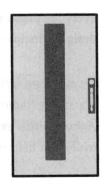

Home Pages

Retail

Professional

Online

Financial

Travel

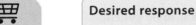
Marketplace

> **Desired response**
> Users understand what you do and click in the right direction to reach their goals.

Your home page is the most coveted piece of your web site's real estate because it is the start page that all users must pass through to use your site. This is where first impressions are formed, but more importantly, it is where your users will orient themselves to click toward their goals. Your home page is like a compass that users will reference to get their bearings and to figure out where to go next. Forget about designing a site map—your home page *is* the site map. With this perspective in mind, your home page should be focused on getting users to see and then click the right path that will lead them toward reaching a mutually desirable goal.

Here are some guidelines to keep in mind as you design your home pages:

- **Home page ≠ splash page.** A *splash page* is usually a branding page that is the first page users see before they gain access to your "real" home page. Splash pages are basically useless; they do nothing for your site except force your users to click through a page they didn't want to see in the first place. When users arrive at your site, they should feel like they have been welcomed inside and can get closer to their goal right away.

- **Introduce yourself.** Your home page needs to introduce your web site to its users. The objective is to confirm to users that they have arrived at the right site and to communicate what your web site can do for them. For more information, see the "Introduce Yourself" section in Chapter 2, "Browsers."

- **List your sections vertically.** Vertical lists of sections are always easier to scan than horizontal ones. Scanning across horizontal lists is more difficult because your eye has to work harder to find the next section, whereas vertical lists are easy to scan down. Compare the following two layouts by trying to locate "Kids Outerwear," and you'll see what I mean:

Layout 1: Horizontal List

Women:	Blouses | Sweaters | Dresses | Pants | Shorts | Skirts
Men:	Dress Shirts | Sweaters | Suits | Jeans | Pants | Shorts | Socks
Kids:	Shirts | Jeans | Pants | Shorts | Outerwear | Socks
Home:	Dining | Kitchen | Living Room | Bath | Storage

Layout 2: Vertical List

Women:	**Men:**	**Kids:**	**Home:**
• Blouses	• Dress Shirts	• Shirts	• Dining
• Sweaters	• Sweaters	• Jeans	• Kitchen
• Dresses	• Suits	• Pants	• Living Room
• Pants	• Jeans	• Shorts	• Bath
• Shorts	• Pants	• Outerwear	• Storage
• Skirts	• Shorts	• Socks	
	• Socks		

- **Explain your main sections or paths.** Don't make the assumption that your users will immediately understand where your main sections or paths will take them. Take, for example, the word "Storage" as a main section title within an office-supplies web site. Does this section refer to paper boxes, office shelving, or hard drives? By including a brief description beside the section name or a list of some of the subsections (as in the preceding example), you can help your users understand know what each section is.

Sephora's home page takes extra care in ensuring that its main sections are seen—they are vertically listed on the left despite also being a part of the top navigation bar.

www.sephora.com

- **Don't make anything look like a banner.** If you have a featured promotion that you want to highlight on your home page, don't make it look anything remotely like a banner. Users have learned to ignore banner ads and anything that looks even closely related to them. If you want your users to see something, the simplest solution is to make it a text link.

- **The home page should be a no-pop-up zone.** The most annoying types of home pages are those that automatically pop-up new browser windows. What's even worse is when users close these pop-ups, navigate into the site, click back to the home page, and the pop-up reappears! If you absolutely must do a pop-up, at least make it so that it only launches on the first time a user enters the home page.

Site Search Pages

> ### Desired response
> Users can easily find what they are looking for.

Retail

Professional

Online

Financial

Travel

Marketplace

A site search enables your users to search for content and products within your site. It's important that you put some care into designing your site search because it really is an alternative way for your users to navigate your site.

Keep these guidelines in mind as you work on designing search pages:

- **By default, search all.** On some larger sites, users are given the capability to select a search zone to enable them to search within a subsection of a site. Although this is fine for users who know which subsection to look into, most users will have no preconceived notion as to where they should search (er…which is why they're using the search feature in the first place), nor should they be required to work to figure out where to search. So, by default, you should allow users to search the entire site.

  Some sites don't preselect the "search all" option to encourage users to select a specific search zone so that the search only looks through a subset of the site's pages and avoids bogging down the server. The flaw in this approach is that your users end up being bogged down because they have to work through additional clicks. Here's a before and after of Monster's job search function in terms of how it should work:

Before

After

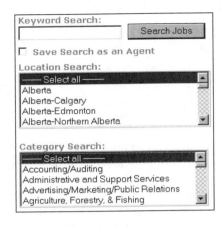

www.monster.com

In the Before version, Monster's job search function requires users to explicitly click the "Select all" option for both the location and the category. For users who return to the site often, this repetitive clicking can become tiresome.

In the modified After version, the "Select all" options are preselected as the default, and the search button is located close to the text field for as little mousing as possible. Although the changes are minor, they do add up for users who use your search again and again.

- **Allow for an iterative search.** When you display your search results, you should redisplay the search text box and have it prefilled with the original search criteria. This will help users remember what they just searched for and will enable them to modify their input (in case there are no matches) and correct any typos.

■ **Differentiate the results.** When you display search results, you need to provide enough information for each result to help your users choose between them. To differentiate the results, you might include items such as a thumbnail photo, short description text, and the section where the item is found. Linking the sections helps users look through related products if nothing in the immediate results is of interest to them.

```
You Searched For:  pants
Results found: eddiebauer.com (123);


eddiebauer.com
Mens (66); Womens (50); On Sale (7);


       Men Five-Pocket Relaxed-Fit Jeans New!                          Product
       Men / Pants & Shorts / Jeans
```

www.eddiebauer.com

Eddie Bauer's search results are differentiated by their descriptions, accompanying thumbnail images, and the category links provided. One improvement in these search results, however, would be to include the price.

Retail

Professional

Financial

Travel

Articles

> **Desired response**
>
> Users view your site as a credible and thorough resource to help them select and purchase related products and services.

Providing good content on your site is like having a knowledgeable staff on your sales floor. Informative articles give your site credibility and help your users feel confident in doing business with you.

These guidelines will be helpful as you design your article pages:

- **Summarize the article at the beginning.** Provide a quick summary of the article's content at the beginning. This will help your users quickly determine whether they should keep reading or move on.

- **Feature the author.** One of the easiest ways to increase the credibility of your content is to feature the author's name and photo with the article. Researchers at Stanford's Persuasive Technology Lab found that there was a significant positive impact on the credibility of a web page if it featured a formal photo (for example, wearing business attire) of the author. The implicit statement behind this is that the author is willing to be identified and thus stands behind the content presented. Extending this thought a little further, you should also include a short author bio and a link to email the author.

- **Provide related links.** Never leave your users hanging—always provide them with a link to the next piece of content, related products or services, or a call to action. Any related links should be placed at the top right of the page so that users can scan the article summary and the related links at the same time to determine whether they should continue reading this page or click to something else. The calls to action should then be repeated at the bottom so that users who are really interested in the topic can respond.

Top

| print this article | email a colleague | send feedback | Read Feedback |

Good Copywriters Deserve More Money
› › › Writing Online

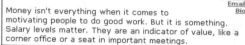

BY Nick Usborne | 12-6-2001

Money isn't everything when it comes to motivating people to do good work. But it is something. Salary levels matter. They are an indicator of value, like a corner office or a seat in important meetings.

nickUSBORNE
Articles
Email
Bio

www.clickz.com

At the ClickZ site, the author photos, bios, and email addresses help enhance the credibility of the articles. Related actions and articles are also presented at the bottom of the page.

Bottom

| print this article | email a colleague | send feedback |

Nick Usborne speaks, writes, and consults on strategic copy issues for business online. See his site for details. For Web sites, emails and newsletters, he crafts messages that drive results. He is the author of the critically acclaimed book *Net Words - Creating High-Impact Online Copy*.

Article Archives by Nick Usborne:

›› Optimize Your Home Page for New Visitors 2-14-2002

›› Not Sure What to Say? Start Writing... 1-31-2002

›› Cynics Can't Write Great Copy 1-17-2002

›› Can Conglomerates Speak in the First Person? 1-3-2002

›› The Power of the First Person 12-20-2001

›› Good Copywriters Deserve More Money 12-6-2001

MORE ...

- **Email it to a friend.** The capability to email an article to a friend is important because a referred page is much more likely to be read by the recipient. Sites that recognize the influential power of referrals even give out rewards to users who forward links on to others. This function is usually found at the bottom of a page and assumes that only users who have read the article would consider forwarding it. Also make sure you state your privacy policy (or a link to it) near where the email address is entered so that referrers will know whether they're adding their friend's email address to a spam database or not.

- **Offer a printer-friendly version.** Having a printer-friendly version of your document is a must (assuming that your default web page layout is not suitable for printing) because it gives users an opportunity to review the content offline or even to bring it with them to a physical store. In keeping with the general rule of avoiding pop-up windows (pop-ups are intrusive unless users explicitly ask for a new window to be opened), you should just link to the printer-friendly version in the same browser window. The items that you should include in your printer-friendly version are as follows:

- The name of the site and its URL.

- Instructions on how to print the page, or a print button that actually prints the page.

- The permanent URL of the article.

- If the article spans a multiple number of web pages, the printer-friendly version should combine all the pages in one page for easy printing.

On the flip side, your main navigation bar and the related links should be removed from the printer-friendly version. Only the article's content and the author's name, bio, and photo should be included with the preceding items.

Anchordesk's printer-friendly versions of its articles include references to where the articles are from and where they are located. This makes it easier for users to go back to the article or the site for more information. Even though this isn't a transaction-oriented site, it's still a good example of a printer-friendly version.

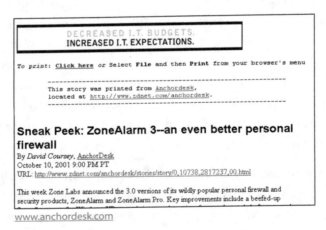

www.anchordesk.com

Product-Listing Pages

Retail

Desired response

Users are able to choose the products you want them to choose.

Product-listing pages display links to products of a particular type. These pages should assist users in choosing between products for further investigation while at the same time influencing them to pick the products that you want them to buy.

Effective product-listing pages will help users choose the right product without having to resort to jumping back and forth between the listing and detail pages. In fact, good product-listing pages should help sell the product prior to the user viewing the details.

Financial

Travel

These ideas will come in handy as you create these pages:

Marketplace

- **Include brief descriptions.** Provide brief, differentiating descriptions of your products right on the product-listing page. Don't just rely on product numbers or codes because these will only be meaningful to your internal staff and your most frequent buyers. Provide enough detail for users to be able to decide which product to click for more information. Make sure you include the price—don't force users to go to the detail page to find out how much an item costs.

www.smartbargains.com

Smartbargains.com's product-listing pages make it easy to differentiate between products and sort them. The integration of product availability ("Only 17 left!") provides further motivation for users to select an item. Also note that for each item, multiple links are provided to access the details (the photo, the description, and "More Info").

- **Integrate price anchoring.** Price anchoring is about influencing users to purchase a particular item given its price. An experiment (by Itamar Simonson and Amos Tversky) was conducted at a Sharper Image store where they featured two breadmakers—one was listed at $200 and the other at $250. With this setup, most shoppers ended up purchasing the $200 model. But when a third breadmaker for $400 was placed along-side the other two models, the $250 model became more popular. By introducing the third, more expensive model, the $250 model suddenly became much more reasonably priced in comparison. On your prod-uct-listing pages, you could feature products that integrate this concept to promote particular products at a given price point.

- **Buy it now.** When users view your product-listing pages, they shouldn't have to click to the product details page to add an item to their shop-ping cart. For users who already know what they want, you should give them quick access to buy the item from the product-listing pages.

- **Allow for sorting.** Sorting provides a quick means for users to zero in on the product they want. Some parameters for sorting include:

    - Featured items (which enables you to feature selected items first as the default sort)

    - Name

    - Brand

    - Price

    - Date (for example, the date released)

    - Best-selling items

    - Percent discount

- **Allow for comparisons.** Product-listing pages are also the appropriate place to let your users select items for comparison. For more about this, see the "Comparing Apples to Apples" section in Chapter 3, "Evaluators."

Product Pages

> **Desired response**
> Users are able to evaluate products so that they can decide to buy them.

Retail

Product pages provide the specific details of a selected item. Predecided transactors use these pages to verify that they've selected the right item. For evaluators who are still deciding, these pages help them decide whether to buy the item or not.

Here are some guidelines to keep in mind as you design your product pages:

Financial

- **Highlight features and benefits.** As previously mentioned in the "It Starts with Great Content" section of Chapter 3, you should highlight both the features and benefits of your product. Make it clear to your users how your product benefits them.

Travel

Marketplace

- **Don't skimp on the details.** When it comes to providing information about a product, don't be afraid to go long on the details. Don't overwhelm your users with paragraphs of text, but do provide an exhaustive bullet-point list about the product. The details should preemptively answer any questions that users are likely to have. Start with the strongest features and the answers to the most frequently asked questions. Motivated users will keep on reading, and the more information you provide them with to chew on, the more committed they can become to buying the product.

- **Photos that provide answers.** For most products, the most useful photos are those that show the product in a way that answers the questions that users are likely to have. For example, I once observed some users visiting a retail-clothing web site that had photographs in which the clothing was laid flat as if on a table. Although the photos were professional and clear, the inevitable question asked was "How does that look on a person?" In this case, the photo didn't really answer the users' primary question.

Photos should also show off the features of the product. If you sell jackets, how will one straight-on photo tell your users that there is an inside pocket? If you're selling cameras, how will users know whether the dials are easy to understand or how big the zoom lens is unless you show them? Don't hesitate to have multiple product shots from different angles and levels of detail to highlight the features that matter most to your users.

When users view the different colors of jackets at Abercrombie & Fitch, they are also shown different product features such as the inside pockets.

www.abercrombie.com

- **Let your users do the talking.** As covered in the section by this name in Chapter 3, you should feature user reviews of your products. Either manually integrate your users' feedback or provide them with the capability to dynamically add their own reviews of products. By doing so, you provide social proof to your users regarding how good or bad the product really is.

The reviews must appear to be real and unbiased and not based on a web site that simply wants to move products. One way that Amazon.com tries to make its users' reviews more credible is by asking reviewers to include their name and where they are from.

> ★★★★★ **A Must Have For All Golfers,** October 10, 2001
> Reviewer: **Brian Rendine (see more about me)** from Dallas, TX USA
> This is an amazing combination of instruction, advice and tips on how to play the great game of golf by it's best player, Tiger Woods. I have read nearly every instructional book every published and this is the best one ever ! Buy it now and start to benefit from Tigers wisdom and insights.

www.amazon.com

User reviews at Amazon.com provide a credible way for evaluators to assess products. By identifying the reviews' authors and where they're from, the reviews becomes much more authentic to visitors.

- **The all-important buy button.** The buy button is your favorite button of all—it's the one that enables users to transact. When users visit any given product page, they should immediately see the buy button without having to scroll. Subtlety is not a virtue here—make sure the buy button is loud and clear. For more on buttons, see the "Buttons" section later in this chapter.

- **Allow for "next" navigation.** If your product is part of a predefined category, you should provide the capability for your users to navigate to the next item in that category. This makes it more convenient for your users to navigate to other related products should the current product not meet their needs. This also makes it easier for users to browse through your products without having to always go back to the product-listing page.

Case Studies

> **Desired response**
>
> Users are convinced of your competency and expertise and have a desire to contact you.

Professional

Financial

Customer case studies are the mainstays of web sites for companies that sell services. These pages provide a summary of a success story that a company has had with one of its clients. Case studies provide the proof to convince prospects that they have found the right solutions provider.

Your customer case study pages will be most effective if you keep these guidelines in mind as you design:

- **Let the client speak.** The most credible witnesses of your service's competencies are your customers. The more you let them make statements about your company, the more credible any claims will be. Letting your clients speak means putting them front and center of the case study. Incorporate elements such as customer testimonials or quotations and include specific details about the customer such as their name and job title (if appropriate). The more real you make your customers, the more real their opinions will be.

Vignette literally lets its clients speak by showcasing video testimonials of their experience. The point here is not necessarily to encourage you to shoot videos of your customers, but you should use them as credible spokespersons on your behalf.

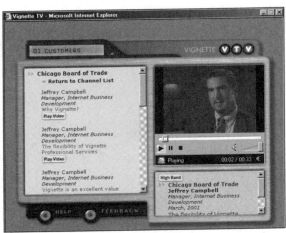

www.vignette.com

- **Use images to make it real.** Although a service isn't a tangible good that you can photograph, it's still important for you to include images in your case study pages to help make the experience more real. Think of a case study as a mini documentary and include the images you would use to convey the story. If you provide financial services, you might include a picture of a couple in front of the new home you helped them finance. If you're an office designer, you might show a before and after of an interior you redesigned. If you're a consultant, you might include a diagram that explains the process that you work through with your clients. In other words, don't just use words to sell your service; use pictures to help your prospects visualize their experience in working with you.

- **Problem, solution, result.** The simplest structure for a case study is problem, solution, and result. Provide a scannable overview (use bullet points, highlight key words) of what the initial problem was, the solution you implemented, and the beneficial result.

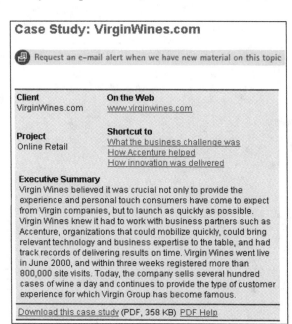

Accenture's case studies provide an executive summary along with shortcuts to "What the business challenge was" (problem), "How Accenture helped" (solution), and "How innovation was delivered" (results). There is also a printable PDF version available.

www.accenture.com

- **Provide a printable version.** Provide a printable, detailed version of the case study so that decision-makers have a takeaway that they can review with others. This is particularly important because decisions often are made in meeting rooms instead of in front of the computer.

- **Prominently display the call to action.** As with the buy button on product pages, make sure you prominently feature your calls to action so that they are visible without requiring users to scroll. If your main call to action is for your users to contact you, incorporate this within the main body of the page—don't just relegate the contact link to the navigation bar.

Buttons

> **Desired response**
>
> Users can recognize your buttons and feel confident to click on them.

Retail

Professional

Online

Financial

Travel

Marketplace

Okay, so buttons aren't pages. They are so important in designing transactional web sites, however, that they warrant having a section of their own. The buttons I will focus on are the ones used to initiate transactions. Poorly designed buttons can lead to lost transactions and lost customers, but effective ones will lead users to click on them.

System Versus Graphic Buttons

The first choice you must make regarding your buttons is whether to use system-based buttons (coded via HTML and rendered by the browser) or graphic buttons (in which you design a graphic image to act as a button). The advantages and disadvantages of each button type are summarized here:

System Buttons	Graphic Buttons
Advantages • These are the most common type of button, and users are familiar with what they look like. • They are easy to implement and change. • They provide visual feedback to let users know that they are being clicked. **Disadvantages** • You have limited control over their size, and they generally can't be used if you have limited space. • They are rendered differently in different browsers and in different operating systems, making it more difficult to control your layout. • You can only change the colors and text of buttons within certain browsers.	**Advantages** • They provide complete control over the look, feel, and size of the button. • They enable you to visually differentiate and prioritize them. • They look the same across all browsers and operating systems. **Disadvantages** • These buttons are graphics, so they do contribute to download time. • Users might not recognize them as buttons (if you don't follow some of the guidelines mentioned in this section). • They don't provide any feedback when clicked (unless you create an alternate image of the button that makes it look clicked and create a JavaScript function to simulate the effect).

If you're pressed for time or lack the appropriate resources, system-generated buttons will always be an acceptable choice. Users are familiar with these buttons because they look the same as other buttons in their operating system. If you have the time and the resources, however, creating image-based buttons will offer you more control and flexibility.

The Art of Making Buttons

Here are some design considerations for creating transactional buttons that lead users to the next step:

- **Make them visible.** For your users to click on your buttons, they must be able to see them first. Buttons should be visible on a page without requiring users to scroll down to see them, and they generally are expected to be found on the right side of the page (because this is where a user's mouse pointer tends to be for scrolling). If your pages are long, you might consider placing a transaction button at the bottom so that it's readily available.

- **Make them clickable.** For system-generated buttons, this is a non-issue because users are already familiar with what they look like and expect them to be clickable. For graphic buttons, it's important that you make your buttons look clickable. The simplest way is to make sure your button is outlined with some shadow or a beveled edge so that it has some depth.

- **Prioritize between buttons.** Not all buttons are created equal, nor should they all look the same. Take a look at the buttons on Wal-Mart's shopping cart. The button for the preferred next step is reversed out to give it more prominence; the secondary buttons are outlined and are slightly smaller. It's okay to have slightly inconsistent buttons to visually prioritize them for users.

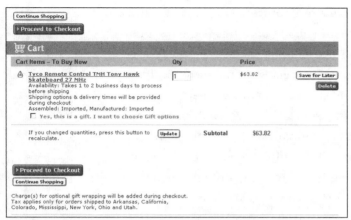

www.walmart.com

In Wal-Mart's shopping cart, the "Proceed to Checkout" button is reversed out and larger than its lesser counterparts. Also notice that the buttons are repeated at the top and bottom of the page.

- **Use descriptive labels.** The labels on your buttons have a significant impact on whether or not they are clicked. The most important aspect of button labels is that they should explain what happens after they are clicked. For example, on a product page, the main transactional button should be something like "Add to Cart." If you use "Buy," some users might think that they will purchase the item immediately. For designers, the meaning of the "Buy" button might be obvious, but for the uninitiated, it might make them hesitate.

- **Provide supporting button text.** Sometimes, in an effort to be descriptive, the most appropriate button label just doesn't fit on a reasonably sized button. If this is the case, consider placing some supporting text just beside the button to better explain how it works.

  Another effective way to use supporting button text is to reassure and encourage users that it's safe to click the button. One way to encourage users is to explain to them that they have a safety net to change their mind about the transaction. By doing this, you help make your users more comfortable about taking the first step toward completing the transaction.

www.sears.com

The "Add to Cart" button at the Sears site reassures users that they can always remove items from their shopping cart later.

- **Never, ever have a reset button.** One of the most useless buttons that I still see on forms is the reset or clear button. These buttons enable the user to wipe out all the information entered on the current form. Why would anyone ever want to do that? I can't ever see a reason why someone would go through the trouble of filling out a form, only to click on the reset button to clear out all the information at the end. What's worse is when this button is right beside the desired action button—users could accidentally click on the wrong button. You might as well label these buttons as "Lost Transactions" for all they're worth.

The Space Coast Credit Union site has a loan application form that is 22 screens long (at 800×600 resolution) and has approximately 218 fields that users can fill out. At the end of this form, there is a "Start Over" button that users can click to clear everything and effectively destroy probably an hour's worth of work—creating an extremely frustrated user.

The "Start Over" button is a time bomb waiting to happen.

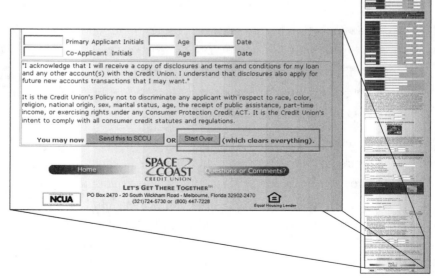

Shopping Cart and Checkout

Desired response
Users are easily able to check out and submit their order.

Retail

Online

Travel

Marketplace

Day after day, web designers hear about how many shopping carts are left abandoned. I believe that users will continue to abandon shopping carts for a number of reasons:

- **They are using the shopping cart as a bookmarking system.** Some users use the shopping cart to create a wish list of items that they want to get. Again, users will abandon these carts because they have no intention of buying.

- **They are using the shopping cart as a calculator.** Many users use the shopping cart just to see how much their total cost will be. Users who use the cart in this way will always abandon it.

- **They get sticker shock.** If you don't tell your users the total cost (including shipping!) until the end, they might be surprised at how much the total order will cost and click away.

- **They get cold feet.** If users aren't completely sold on the products they have added to their shopping carts, they will abandon them. These shoppers might have an unanswered product question or a lingering concern about the site's policies that only manifests itself when users are asked to commit. The solution is to address users' concerns up front by providing more complete product-information pages.

- **They get scared about entering their credit cards online.** This is the hardest hurdle to overcome, and some users will just never feel comfortable submitting their credit card numbers online. The best you can do is provide information about the security precautions that you've taken but also provide an alternate means for users to order from you (such as a toll-free number).

Your best bet is to provide shopping carts that are quick and easy to use and help your users feel like they are in control. Use the following guidelines to make sure your shopping cart and checkout pages help your users submit their orders:

- **Make it clear that items have been added.** Once I visited a retail site where I went to a product page, clicked on the Add to Shopping Cart button, the page refreshed, and I was brought back to what appeared to be the same product page. As I stared at the screen, expecting some sort of confirmation, I could not immediately see that my item had been added. Upon closer inspection, I finally noticed a small space at the bottom of the page that had a summary of my shopping cart contents in type so small that I ended up bumping my nose against the screen while trying to read it. Ugh.

  When your users add something to their shopping carts, make sure you make it absolutely clear to them that the item has been added. If you use a persistent shopping cart that displays its contents and follows users as they navigate the site, make sure you have a very bold and strong indicator that items have been added. Otherwise, users might inadvertently add the same item multiple times and end up becoming bulk buyers of Imodium.

  A simpler alternative to a persistent cart is to link users to the contents of the shopping cart each time they add an item.

- **Provide links back to the product.** Make it easy for your users to go back to their selected products so that they can verify that they've selected the right items. In every case, the product name (and an accompanying image, if applicable) should be linked.

- **Estimate the total cost.** One of the main reasons for abandoned shopping carts is that the total cost of the order wasn't conveyed beforehand. When your users are viewing their shopping carts, they should be able to at least get an estimate of their taxes and shipping costs instead of waiting until the final confirmation.

www.bluelight.com

bluelight.com's shopping cart has many features that make it an excellent example: The product name links back to the product, shipping and handling is estimated, users are given options to continue shopping in related sections, links to supporting information are provided (at the top) to enable users to feel comfortable with shopping online, and a toll-free customer service phone number is provided.

- **Enable users to continue shopping.** To maximize your order sizes, you should provide a convenient link for your users to continue shopping, but you should make it less prominent relative to the Proceed to Checkout button.

  Don't make the mistake of linking the Continue Shopping button back to the home page. This would be the equivalent of being transported to the front of a store each time you added something to a real-life shopping cart! Instead, you should provide a brief list of the most recently visited sections so that users can go back and shop some more.

- **Sign in to check out.** When users click on the option to check out, they usually are presented with a screen that asks them either to sign in if they already have an account or to identify themselves as new customers.

  Let's take a look at a before and after of the Barnes & Noble web site's sign-in to see how you shouldn't and should design this type of page.

www.bn.com

This page might seem simple enough, but there is a problem with it. The fault of this design is that new users are placed second. When users arrive at a page, they tend to go to the first thing that makes sense for them to fill in. In this case, new and existing users alike will start filling in their email address in the Returning Customers area on the left. The problem is further compounded by some users who will enter their email password because they won't realize that they have to enter a password created specifically for this site. New users will then receive an error message because they haven't created their account yet, and they could end up leaving in frustration.

Now let's take a look at what Barnes & Noble did to improve their sign-in page:

After

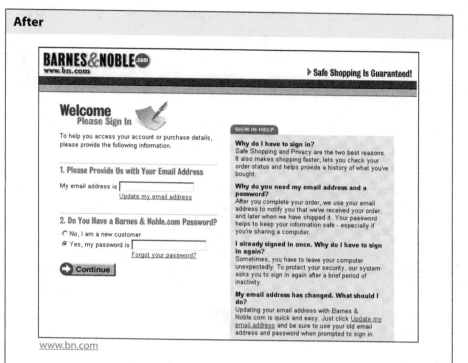

www.bn.com

This design has been improved significantly because it consolidates the sign-in for both new and returning users. The old design relied too heavily on assuming that users would read the whole page prior to entering their information, when in fact they usually started filling out the first thing that made sense to them. Another improvement is that the sign-in explicitly asks for users' Barnes & Noble password so that they don't confuse it with their personal email password. Finally, the explanatory text on the right can only make users (especially new ones) feel more comfortable with the sign-in process and why it is necessary.

- **You shouldn't have to register just to buy something.** As previously mentioned, don't force your users to register for an account before they can check out. Instead, allow all users to go through the checkout process and then, at the end, provide them with the option to create an account to store their information.

- **Ask for the payment at the end.** There are a few reasons why you should ask for payment at the end. The first reason is that it's what users expect to do at the conclusion of a transaction. When users enter their payment information, they feel like they've paid for the product. The second reason is a practical one: Suppose you collect payment information first and then shipping information second. If anything were to go wrong with collecting the shipping information, users would feel like they were stuck with an undeliverable product that they just paid for. A third reason is that users are most committed at the end because they've just entered all of their information and therefore will be more inclined to complete the transaction.

- **Include an order-confirmation page.** The order-confirmation page should list all of the information entered by your users and enable them to edit any inputs or preferences. The only exception is that you should mask out (replace the digits with asterisks) all but the last four digits of the credit-card number (so that users can identify the card).

Amazon.com takes a novel approach by taking repeat customers directly to a summary confirmation page with their default address, payment, and shipping options prefilled rather than requiring users to navigate through the whole checkout process.

When returning customers check out of Amazon's shopping cart, they are brought directly to a confirmation page with their default options already entered. A big "Place your order" button is featured to make sure users can't miss it.

www.amazon.com

- **Have a big submit order button.** The most important button you'll ever design on your e-commerce site is the one that finally submits your users' orders. Make this button big, bold, and unavoidable. Repeat it at the top and the bottom of your screen and communicate to your users that the order isn't received until they click that button.

Application Forms

> **Desired response**
>
> Users feel safe to fill out and submit their application.

Application forms are used to apply for products such as mortgages or to open accounts. For financial-services sites, application forms are the equivalent of shopping carts for retail sites—but these forms can be just as easily abandoned if you're not careful with their design.

These ideas will help you make sure your applications are as painless as possible for your users:

- **Allow for alternate channels.** Sometimes going online isn't the best way to get something done. This can be particularly true for a long application form/process. Sometimes paper or even the phone might be a more efficient way to apply. Your users might also be uncomfortable with submitting personal information online, so in any case, it's best to provide them with alternative channels to apply.

During the application process, Chase provides users with alternative channels for completing the application.

www.chase.com

- **Set expectations up front.** One way to completely frustrate your users is to have them start filling out your application form and then find out that they're missing a key piece of information or that they don't have enough time to finish it. You can prevent this frustration by clearly setting expectations up front. These expectations should be included as an introductory page before users actually start the form and should include the following:

- **Explain any special information requirements.** List any special pieces of information that a person might not normally have with her. Keep in mind that many users might be completing the form at work and that a lot of their personal information might be at home.

- **Set a time expectation.** Explain how long an application typically will take to complete.

- **Explain the process.** Explain to your users what will happen after they submit the form. Set the expectation as to whether they will be immediately notified regarding approval or will have to wait for a later response.

- **Include any disqualifiers.** If there are any required prerequisites for your users, state them up front so that people don't waste their time filling out a form for something they don't qualify for (for example, the product or service is only available for a specific geographic location).

www.bankamerica.com

At the Bank of America site, users are prequalified before they start any application forms. Time commitments and information require-ments are clearly laid out so that users who start the form will stand a better chance of finishing.

- **Funnel the navigation.** When users are filling out your application form, you want them to focus on applying. The way to do this is to remove your site's main navigation bar and not include any links that will take the user out of the form. The only way out of the form should be if the user clicks on a Cancel button.

- **Put the cursor in the first form field.** For each page of the form, you should code your HTML so that the cursor is preselected in the first form field. This will make things just a little bit easier for users by minimizing the amount of mousing they have to do.

- **Show progress.** Filling out an application form can feel like walking in the desert—users keep going but don't see any end in sight. If your form is made up of multiple steps, you should provide a progress bar or numbered steps (for example, "You are on step 3 of 5") to help users feel like they're going forward and that there's a specific ending point. Be cautious about using numbered steps, however, if your form has multiple branches that might yield a changing number of steps depending on the options that users select.

- **Test out your tab order.** The tab order is the order in which users advance through form fields by pressing the Tab key on their keyboards. Most users filling out an application form will be looking at their keyboard as they type and will assume that the Tab key will place them in the next logical field. Trouble can occur if you don't code the tab order into your HTML; your users might be brought to an unexpected field and tell you that their last name is New York. On the other hand, you should also avoid automatically tabbing users to the next field because they don't expect forms to behave in this manner.

- **Get rid of any optional fields.** This is just a reminder not to be tempted to collect any marketing information from your users as they fill out your forms. Collecting marketing information up front sends up a red flag for users: "Are they interested in serving me, or do they just want to get as much out of me as possible?" Your first priority is to get these users to be your customers—not part of your focus group.

- **Integrate help and reassurance text.** As users fill out an application form, they might come across questions that they either don't know how to answer or don't want to fill out. For some questions, you might need to integrate some help text to guide users as to how to answer them. For more sensitive pieces of information (for example, a social security number), you might need to include reassurances about your security precautions as well as a brief explanation of why the information is necessary and how it will be used. Ultimately, the best way to find out where users need some supporting text is to test out the application form.

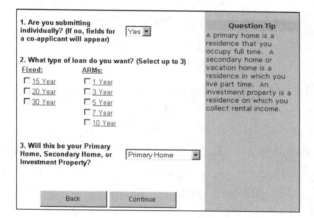

Bank of America's mortgage application provides Question Tips to help users select and provide the right answers to questions.

- **Provide a lifeline.** Whether it is a phone number or online chat, it's important to provide users with live help to address any spur-of-the-moment questions they might have as they are filling out the forms. Make sure you include the hours and the time zone for when support is available.

- **Provide a confirmation page.** The final step for your application form should be to enable users to verify that they've entered the correct information. The confirmation page should redisplay all of the information in the same order and groupings as the user entered it. If your form is made of multiple pages, the groupings should be according to these pages. Each grouping should have an edit button that leads users back to that particular page of the form (with the entered values already prefilled) to enable users to modify their inputs. When these users continue, they should be brought straight back to the confirmation page.

Confirmation pages should also make it clear that they are not the end of the process. Many users need to be reminded that they need to submit the form to finalize the process.

- **Only use "Submit" at the end.** If your application form consists of multiple steps, make sure you label only the last button in the final confirmation step with something like "Submit." The term "Submit" should only be used when the form is actually being sent. All other buttons that just lead the user to the next step should be labeled as either "Next" or "Continue."

- **Confirm the receipt.** As a final reassurance, provide a page that confirms that you've received the user's application(s). If any financial transaction was involved, you should display a confirmation number. This page should explain any next steps and should provide information on how to get support or pursue further inquiries. For more information, see "The Online Receipt" section in Chapter 5, "Customers."

Error Pages

> **Desired response**
> Users are able to recover from errors and finish their transactions.

Retail

Professional

Online

Financial

Travel

Marketplace

Error pages aren't really separate pages on their own, but they're so often overlooked that they need special attention. I've found that site designers tend to focus on the "happy path" in which users always figure out how to use forms and fill them out correctly on the first try. Despite your best efforts, errors will still be made, and you need to provide the proper safety net for users to be able to recover and continue with the transaction.

One of the first things you should do in designing any interactive form is figure out how errors will be handled. There are four ways in which you can display error messages:

- **A separate error page.** This is perhaps the easiest option to implement—the user is brought to a separate page that displays what went wrong. Although this might be easier to develop, it's the hardest type of error handling for your users because it requires them to make note of what went wrong and remember it as they go back and correct what they did incorrectly. This might be one of the quickest ways to handle errors, but it is also the dirtiest.

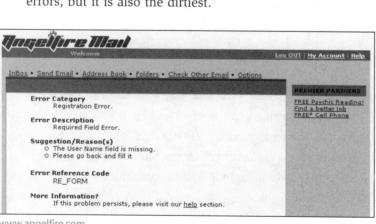

www.angelfire.com

Angelfire's free email registration form displays its error messages (which are unfortunately cryptic) on a separate page.

- **JavaScript error alerts.** These error messages are relatively quick and easy to implement provided you're familiar with making JavaScript work across various browsers and platforms. The advantage of this method is that the error messages are instant—they don't require users to go to another page, and they avoid sending more requests to the server. JavaScript error checking is most useful for verifying the presence and formatting of required fields.

  One disadvantage of JavaScript alerts is that users must dismiss the pop-up alert before they can continue on with the form. This requires the user to remember what the pop-up message said. Another disadvantage is that only one error message can be displayed at a time, and this can become quite painstaking if there are multiple errors. A final disadvantage is that these error messages are directly embedded in the HTML pages, making them a bit more difficult to centralize and manage for consistency.

Mail.com's registration form makes use of JavaScript error alerts that check for errors before the information is even sent to the server.

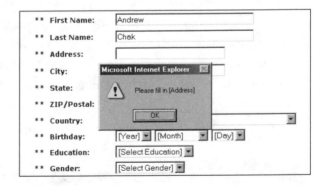

- **Inline error messages.** These error messages are directly integrated with the form page that the error is on. The best practice is to clearly state at the top of the page (usually in red) that there is an error and to tell the user to look for any errors throughout the page. Every field with an error should be highlighted and accompanied by explanatory text for how to fix the problem.

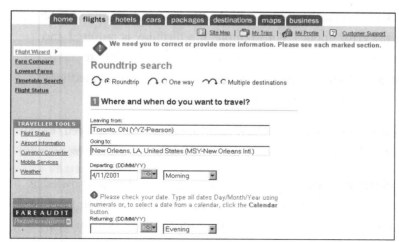

Expedia's flight-search form utilizes inline error messages to make it easy for users to find out what's wrong with the information they entered.

www.expedia.com

- **Only what's wrong.** This last option is the most complex to implement, but it also provides the most guidance to your users when filling out a form. This type of error handling is most preferred for longer registration forms, and it's a good investment if your site only has one main call to action.

This error-handling method is similar to the inline method except that instead of redisplaying the entire page, the user is presented only with the fields that have a problem. Hotmail provides an excellent example of this:

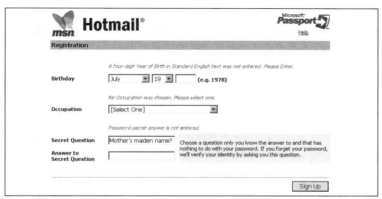

Hotmail provides a very robust error-handling mechanism that redisplays only the necessary fields to help a user properly fill out his membership application form. If there is a problem with a particular field, all of its related fields are also redisplayed.

www.hotmail.com

- **Communicate what has gone wrong.** Explain to users that you can't find the page they're looking for—this way, you take ownership for the problem, and you reassure the users that it's not their fault. Explain to them that they should double-check the URL for any typos and that they might be accessing a page that no longer exists due to recent site updates.

- **Help them get on their way.** Your "Page not found" page should include any combination of the following to help users get on their way:

  - Your site search.

  - A site map or an overview of your main site sections. This is particularly important if your site has just undergone a redesign and you need to help reorient users.

  - A link back to your home page so that users can start drilling back down into the site again.

CNET's "Page not found" page is very short and sweet and provides convenient links to help users get back on track.

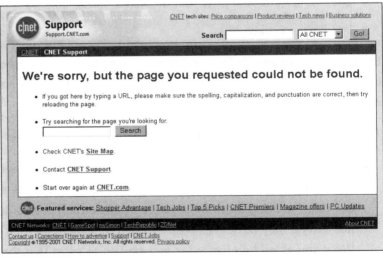

www.cnet.com

Contact Us

> **Desired response**
>
> Users can get in touch with you through their preferred means.

Retail

Professional

Online

Financial

Travel

Marketplace

For many designers, their first thought in terms of a Contact Us page is simply a "mailto:" email link. This is simple and convenient and enables you to manage your responses back to your users. The web is not an island, however; we still live in the real world, and sometimes people want real-world contact. In the same vein, your contact page shouldn't just be an email link; it should include all the channels through which your users can reach you.

The following sections discuss all the different contact channels you might support and provide some guidelines for each.

Email

Users are likely to use email to contact you, but they will welcome information on how to approach you.

- **Explicitly spell out your email address.** Your link to your email address should be something like info@domain.com rather than just Send us an email. This makes it more convenient for users to remember the address should they need it in the future.

- **Set expectations for response time.** State how soon you will be able to respond to the user. The usual expectation is that you'll respond within 24 hours or one business day.

- **Provide separate email addresses for subdepartments.** If multiple areas are charged with answering email, provide an overview of what each of these departments does. Whenever possible, include the names of your contacts; this will help your users feel confident that their inquiries will be taken care of. Also make sure to include a general support address if none of the specific departments seems to apply to the user's query.

■ **Explain what should and should not be sent via email.** Remind users not to send any personal information (such as credit card or account numbers) via email because it is not a secure channel.

Lighthousebank's "Contact Us" page provides multiple channels for its users.

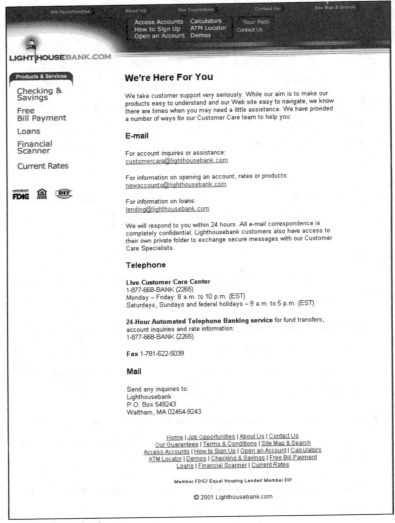

www.lighthousebank.com

Phone (and Fax)

For many users, the phone is still how they prefer to do business.

- **Include your area code and any international prefixes.** Not everyone will be calling from your backyard, so don't forget to explicitly include your area code and international prefixes. If you have a toll-free number, indicate from where it can be used but also provide a non-toll-free number.

- **State your hours of operation.** Tell your users when they can call in, and don't forget to include your time zone.

Addresses and Locations

Sometimes the call to action is to schedule an onsite visit or to mail in an application form. By providing the right address and location information, you can prevent your users from getting lost when trying to find you.

- **Specify the hours of operation for each location.** This helps users know when to call in or when they can schedule an appointment.

- **Include the address and phone number.** The phone number is particularly helpful for users who get lost on their way to your location.

- **Provide a map to the location.** If you don't have the means to create your own map, link to one via MapQuest < www.mapquest.com > or MapBlast < www.mapblast.com > .

- **Provide directions from multiple starting points.** Your directions should accommodate users from multiple starting points such as the airport, downtown, and via public transportation. An nice touch would be to include the average travel time from each starting point.

The directions to this local church are provided from multiple starting points (including public transportation, which is not shown here). The directions are very driver friendly because they provide turning instructions along with the direction they are heading (for example, "Turn left [east]") to help everyone get to church on time!

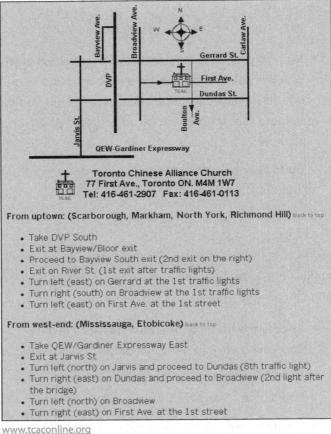

Toronto Chinese Alliance Church
77 First Ave., Toronto ON. M4M 1W7
Tel: 416-461-2907 Fax: 416-461-0113

From uptown: (Scarborough, Markham, North York, Richmond Hill) back to top

- Take DVP South
- Exit at Bayview/Bloor exit
- Proceed to Bayview South exit (2nd exit on the right)
- Exit on River St. (1st exit after traffic lights)
- Turn left (east) on Gerrard at the 1st traffic lights
- Turn right (south) on Broadview at the 1st traffic lights
- Turn left (east) on First Ave. at the 1st street

From west-end: (Mississauga, Etobicoke) back to top

- Take QEW/Gardiner Expressway East
- Exit at Jarvis St.
- Turn left (north) on Jarvis and proceed to Dundas (8th traffic light)
- Turn right (east) on Dundas and proceed to Broadview (2nd light after the bridge)
- Turn left (north) on Broadview
- Turn right (east) on First Ave. at the 1st street

www.tcaconline.org

- **Make your directions printer and driver friendly.** When it comes to designing your directions page, think of someone who has never been to your city and who is driving a rental car by herself at night. With this in mind, you should make your directions printable, and you might want to enlarge your fonts a bit so that it's easier for lone drivers to read the printout as they are driving.

- **Specify any special addressees.** Make sure you specify any special mailing addresses that you might have. For example, a bank might have a special address for receiving application forms, whereas a retail site might have a different address for handling returns.

The Keep-in-Touch Email

> **Desired response**
> Users are drawn back to your site again and again.

Retail

Professional

Online

Financial

Travel

Marketplace

Although emails aren't web pages, as far as the Internet is concerned, the web and email are equal parts in the online experience. Email, however, is much more pervasive (I bet you know more people who use the Internet to check their email than to just surf the web) and is also much more personal (users will take much more ownership over their email than a web page any day). Users won't necessarily check out your web site on a regular basis, but they will check their email. For many companies and web sites, email is the only direct communication link they have with their customers. This is why you need to send out email every so often to keep in touch with customers and draw them back to your site. Use the guidelines presented in this section along with those presented in the "Set Up the Next Transaction" section in Chapter 5.

The following guidelines will help you make the most out of your keep-in-touch emails.

Subject Lines

The subject line of your message might be more important than you think—a few words can mean the difference between a customer reading or trashing your note.

- **Emphasize a reward or a punishment.** Provide a reason for your users to open the email. For example, "Get a 10% discount before October 15th" is much more effective than "Check out our fall sale" because the former contains both a reward (a 10% discount) and a punishment (after October 15th, the discount is no longer available).

Contents

The contents of your email need to engage users to be read and should motivate them to click at the same time.

- **Use "you" as soon as possible.** Make the email centered on your users and their benefits as opposed to yourself.

- **Explain why they're receiving this email.** Remind your users that they're receiving the email as a result of their earlier request.

- **Start off with a summary.** Summarize the key points in the email so that your users can jump to whichever section interests them.

- **Place the most important items first.** Prioritize your key message as the first item of the email and ask for a call to action as soon as possible.

- **Link 'em back to your site.** Always, always provide links back to your site throughout and at the end of the email.

Formatting

By following some simple guidelines for formatting your emails, you can make sure your users see them as they were intended to appear.

- **Provide an alternative to HTML.** If you decide to send your emails in HTML, you ought to include a link to a web page containing the exact same page on your web site. This is for users who have email programs that cannot read HTML emails.

- **Format for 68 characters wide.** Most email readers can properly read email that is 68 characters wide or fewer. To guarantee your formatting, make sure you place hard returns after each line.

- **Put http:// in front of your URLs.** This will ensure that all of your URLs are linked in your users' email readers. For AOL users, you would code a link in HTML (i.e., you need to use an < A HREF > tag around the text).

- **Be mindful of long URLs.** If your URL is longer than 68 characters, it will word wrap within some of your users' email readers and render the link broken. In this case, you should provide alternate instructions in terms of how to access the URL.

> There are TWO different ways to pick up your card:
>
> 1) point your web browser to:
>   http://cgi.cardmaster.com/cgi-bin/get?1234567
>   or
> 2) point your web browser to:
>   http://www.cardmaster.com/my.htm
>   and then enter the 7-digit code: 1234567

www.cardmaster.com

Although its URLs are short, the Cardmaster site sends emails containing alternate methods for accessing its electronic cards in case the URLs get broken up.

- **Don't use BCC.** Don't send your emails all at once using BCC (blind carbon copy) to hide the addresses. Some email sites or applications (such as Hotmail) automatically filter out BCC emails as junk mail, and they may never catch the eye of your users.

Administration

Make it easy for your users to administer their email preferences.

- **Always explain how to unsubscribe.** Provide a clear explanation to your users as to how they can stop receiving these emails.

- **Links to privacy policy.** Reinforce the fact that the email you've sent is adhering to the privacy policy to which they've agreed.

- **Tell them the email address that is being subscribed.** This is helpful for users who pick up their email through other email accounts (for example, via web-based email). It helps them figure out which email address is subscribed.

7

Clicking It Together

Now you've seen them all—browsers, evaluators,

transactors, and customers—four users that I

hope will change how you view your web site.

Now that you understand each of these users, it's

time to bring them together and show you exam-

ples of sites that effectively reach these different

users and funnel them toward transacting.

This chapter will take a look at sample sites for each of the six verticals that have been used throughout this book. The sites chosen are each persuasive in their own right, but keep in mind that what works for one type of site might not work for others. You can also learn from other verticals—don't just limit yourself to reviewing the site that's closest to yours. Your site might span multiple verticals, depending on various subsections of functionality. (For example, a bank's web site might fit well under financial services, but its online banking component could leverage principles from the online services vertical.)

The emphasis on these sites is in the functionality and content they provide to make them persuasive. Although for the most part these sites might be considered "usable," they were primarily chosen for the way they support users to make a decision to transact. Keep in mind that these sites will be updated and, hopefully, improved—but they were selected at this point in time to provide examples of what's done well right now.

Each of these sites, however, has its own strengths and weaknesses. From the viewpoint of our four user types—browsers, evaluators, transactors, and customers—some sites better cater to certain types of users than others. Depending on its goals, not every site is good at (or even needs to be good at) supporting each type of user. In this chapter, you'll notice that some or all of the four user types are present at the beginning of each web site example to indicate which types of users the web site does a good job of supporting.

An Easy-to-Choose Bank

Featured Site: FleetBoston Financial < www.fleet.com >

Users

Browsers   *Evaluators*   *Transactors*   *Customers*

Financial

Bank sites don't have to be like banks. Granted, they need to maintain some sense of conservatism to be credible, but that doesn't mean they have to generic, legalistic, or vanilla. FleetBoston Financial's web site is one that provides a helpful experience for browsers, evaluators, transactors, and customers, and it all starts at the home page.

Simple Paths for Users

FleetBoston's home page is divided into two areas: The main area (occupying the left and center of the screen) is for browsers and evaluators, and the right "action" column is for transactors and customers.

The main area makes it easy for browsers to choose a path because there are only four options. This page isn't cluttered with featured links to the business units with the most clout, special promotions on low-rate credit cards, or the latest press releases on who was just promoted to senior vice president. It's not that these things are always bad, but by removing the clutter, FleetBoston makes it easier for its users to head down the right path.

Another reason this home page works is because its users fall into distinct market segments whose needs don't overlap. It makes sense for users to be able to identify themselves as either personal, small-business, or corporate users. If this were a travel site, however, you wouldn't want users to have to specify whether they were business or leisure travelers because they probably would just want to see what flights were available.

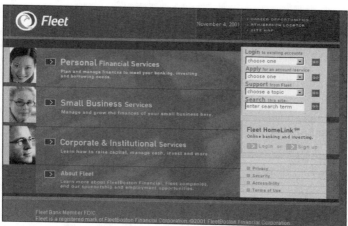

By predominantly featuring only four choices, the FleetBoston home page makes it easier for users to choose the right path.

www.fleet.com

The right column features links to a number of calls to action, including applying for accounts and finding customer support information. Featuring these links on the home page makes it easier for returning transactors to be able to apply without having to dig into the site.

Goals Help Browsers Get Started

When users click on the home page link to Personal Financial Services, they are brought to this page:

Notice how this page follows a center-left-right scan pattern. The first thing users see in the center is the Life Happens section that features articles to help users meet their financial goals. The left column contains links to products, and the right column remains consistent as a call-to-action or next-steps area.

What's refreshing about this page is the emphasis on articles to help users meet their financial goals rather than just generic links to product descriptions. These articles provide a context for introducing browsers to products they might not otherwise consider. For example, browsers who read the article on "Planning for Emergencies" are introduced to FleetBoston's estate-planning services. These goal-based articles are good starting points to help browsers realize their unmet needs.

Helping Evaluators Pick Products

One of the most irritating characteristics of some bank sites is that they just list their products with the assumption that users will understand the difference between a Gold account and a Premier account. The last thing users want to do is unnecessarily surf through a bank's list of product descriptions to find the one that suits their needs.

At the FleetBoston site, however, the first page of the Checking products section is an overview that helps users figure out the difference between products such as their Classic and Self-Service accounts. The overview explains which accounts meet specific needs and summarizes the account features. This makes it easier for users to differentiate between accounts and select the right one to investigate further.

			FleetBoston's checking account overview page makes it easy for users to quickly evaluate and select products.
An affordable checking account relationship that links to your other accounts for simplicity and easy money management **Open a FleetOne Classic account** by April 30, 2002 and enjoy: • **No** minimum balances • **No** monthly fees • **No** transaction fees* • **Free** online banking, including online bill payment **All yours** for the first three months *Certain fees, such as fees for transactions at non-Fleet ATMs and point of sale fees associated with your Fleet 24-Hour Access Card will apply. Owners of non-Fleet ATMs may charge for use of their ATMs.	FleetOne Classic® • Monthly fees of just $10 or $8 with direct deposit waived with a combined minimum average daily balance of at least $4,000 in your linked checking, savings and money market accounts, $2,500 in your Regular Checking account or $3,000 in your Interest Checking account • No transaction fees if minimum balance is maintained • Consolidated monthly statement	• Free access to account information and transfers with Fleet HomeLink[SM] online banking, and Online Bill Payment for just $4.50 a month (free for the first three months after you initiate your first bill payment)[4] • The Fleet Total Access Card (Debit Card) for purchases and ATM access[3] • No annual fee Fleet credit card[2]	
Tailored for those who prefer to bank electronically, by ATM, phone or online	Self Service Checking • Monthly fee of $7 or $5 with Direct Deposit • Unlimited electronic transactions • 20 checks per month and $.50 per check thereafter • $2 for each staff-assisted transaction by phone or in a branch that could have been done electronically[5]	• Free access to account information and transfers with Fleet HomeLink[SM] online banking, and Online Bill Payment for just $4.50 per month (free for the first three months after you initiate your first bill payment)[4] • No minimum balance requirements • A Fleet Total Access Card (Debit Card)[3]	

When users click to view a product, they are presented with a well-designed product page that really helps evaluators decide on the product. Bullet-point summaries are at the top of each product page to highlight the most important product features. Related products and accounts are on the right, and evaluators who want more advanced tools can access calculators and account selectors.

The calls to action remain on the right, but there are also product-specific responses in the middle column just under the product information. The responses range from applying for the product to calling FleetBoston for more information, and users are allowed to respond according to where they are in their decision-making.

Eddie Bauer's home page is very functional yet uncluttered.

www.eddiebauer.com

Next on the home page agenda are the photos. There are simple, primary images: a woman, a man, and a gift. Like storefront mannequins, these images convey to users what they can expect to find inside. It's important for your images to be inclusive of your main types of products so that users can immediately tell what's available at the site.

The featured text links are next. Text links are important because users have learned to look for them to click on. In fact, if you want to attract users to special promotions, you should use text links instead of any banner-like images that users have learned to ignore. Eddie Bauer's featured text links make use of this strategy, but they could be improved slightly by including bullet points to clearly delineate one featured link from the next.

The right side is where users will find some key calls to action such as signing up for email updates or requesting a catalog. Further text-based promotions are displayed along with a link to a gift finder at the bottom. The placement of this gift finder makes an implicit statement, saying, "If you haven't found anything that's of interest on the rest of this page, try the gift finder."

At the very top of the page, you'll notice a utility area that includes links to items such as shopping carts and order status. This top area is reserved exclusively for the current customer. What's nice about the links is that they are fully labeled in terms of tasks. For example, the links are labeled "View Your Shopping Cart" and "Track Your Order Status," rather than just "Shopping Cart" and "Order Status," respectively.

Finally, additional utility links can be found at the very bottom of the page. These links are for those users who didn't find anything of interest at the top and middle of the page. Corporate information is linked here, which makes sense because users who are interested in this information are more motivated to look for it. Alternative shopping methods (such as store or catalog) are also provided here in case users aren't comfortable with online shopping. Next are the online shopping tools, which feature special help to get users started with shopping, and finally, some additional links are provided to help users navigate around the site.

Browsable Product Sections

The first subsection in the main women's section is "Top Sellers," and it's a wonder why more sites don't follow this approach. Think about it: Items that are top sellers are the ones most people might be interested in, so that's why they should be the first link in the section. Furthermore, for the casual browser, these top sellers provide social proof as to what the user should consider buying.

Top Sellers is the first featured subsection within the main women's section. The text view (top image) is presented by default, but users can also switch to the photo-based view (bottom image).

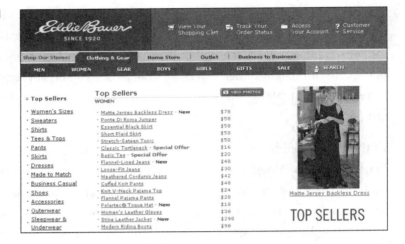

As browsers navigate deeper through the product listings, they are given textual links to products to make page download times faster and thus allow these users to navigate more quickly. There is, however, an alternative view in which users can select to browse items by images. In some sections, such as furniture, Eddie Bauer has cleverly reversed the default to browse by images. Descriptive textual links are fine for distinguishing between a short plaid skirt and corduroy jeans, but the majority of users

Eddie Bauer's "Mix & Match" section helps evaluators find the perfect skirt to go with that blouse.

Prefilling Information for Customers

One of the things that the Eddie Bauer folks hope for, of course, is that visitors will create a user account. The initial setup is a one-step process in which users provide their name, email address, and password. When registered users decide to purchase and check out, their names and email addresses will be prefilled. As users fill out their shipping address and payment information, these items are added to their profile. The site's approach is to only ask for information that is relevant to the current task while incrementally storing information to prefill future transactions.

The "Create an Account" page reminds users of the benefits they receive for signing up.

Customers Get Some Help

The help section features four types of help: a searchable database of questions and answers, live online chat, email, and phone number.

The searchable database is called "Instant Help," and it enables users to navigate through categories of questions and answers. They also can directly enter a free-form question such as "What is your return policy?" If the free-form question doesn't match anything in the database, users are advised to rephrase their question or send it in via email.

As a side note, you should also strongly consider allowing users to search for support information (or at least be redirected to it) through the product search engine. Users don't make a distinction between various internal search engines on your site, so you might want to map words like "return policy" to lead users to your help section.

The live online chat enables users to get their questions answered in real time. Online chat makes it easier for users to ask quick questions, and it is particularly important for users who need help to complete a purchase. Email is too delayed; by the time a response is provided, the user might have bought from elsewhere. By having a variety of help systems, Eddie Bauer can make sure its customers are happy.

Picture-Perfect Acquisitions

Featured Site: Shutterfly < www.shutterfly.com >

Users

Online

Browsers

Evaluators

Transactors

Customers

Online service sites want you to sign up. They want you to become a member, start using the service, and hopefully conduct revenue-generating transactions. This is true whether you're promoting online banking, web-based email, or online storage space. This is also true for digital photo-processing sites such as Shutterfly.

Shutterfly's objective is to get users to upload their digital photos and order prints of them. From your first bad haircut to the fashion crimes of your youth, Shutterfly wants to be the digital photo processor of choice. To meet this objective, Shutterfly needs to do two things: first, get users to sign up to become a member, and second, get them to order prints.

The Simplest of Home Pages

Like the FleetBoston site, Shutterfly's home page is a testament to simplicity. Its first goal is to communicate that it's a digital photo-processing site. This is done through the tagline sentence underneath the logo as well as the prominent image of a woman holding up a print. The second goal of the home page is to get users to sign up. Browsers who are new to the site can choose to "Learn More;" transactors can access the "Sign Up" link right away.

www.shutterfly.com

Shutterfly's home page makes it easy for users to choose between learning more and signing up to become a member.

One interesting thing to note about this home page, however, is the minimal space devoted to returning customers/members. In the top-right corner is a link to "Member Sign In" that enables customers to log in. Part of the reason for such a small link is probably because Shutterfly wants to emphasize acquiring new members. Another reason why Shutterfly can get away with this, however, is that returning customers will expect a login area and will be more motivated to find it. Compare this with relatively unmotivated browsers and evaluators who are still expecting the site to cater to them before they decide to sign up.

Evaluators Learn More

Clicking on the link to "Learn More" provides users with a one-page explanation of how the service works. Again, the simplicity and brevity of the design is what makes this page work. After users quickly scan the explanation, they are asked to respond in some way through the links on the right. The links, however, seem to have been carefully selected and purposefully sequenced to bring users of varying interest levels one step closer to signing up.

The first call to action is the desired one: Sign Up Now. If users have any reservations, they can check out the member benefits right underneath. If this doesn't work, Shutterfly tries to interest users in exploring an interactive tour of the site. Users who are more detail oriented can explore the details of the service instead. Finally, if users aren't interested in learning about the service, Shutterfly provides resources on how to take better pictures in the hopes that this will make users more amenable to the site and give them a reason to stay. From then on, the page works its way down the links, trying to provide something relevant for all users. Imagine that the links on the page were being served up by a salesperson. The conversation would sound something like this:

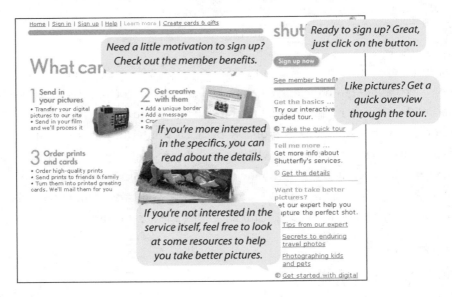

Touring the Site

Tours are important. No online service site should be without one. Not having a visual tour for an online service is like promoting a movie without a trailer or asking someone to buy a car without taking a test drive.

Shutterfly's tour is easy to navigate and enables users to get an interactive preview of its photo-editing features.

Shutterfly's tour is very visual, simple, and interactive. As users step through the tour, they can also click on interactive links that showcase the editing capabilities of the service. Features such as cropping photos, correcting red eye, and adding decorative borders are demonstrated. The point of having a tour is to let evaluators envision what it's like to use the service. The tour's purpose is not to enumerate its features and benefits but to let the evaluator infer them after seeing the service in action. When your users say to themselves, "Hey, I could do this!" they are halfway toward signing up.

Signing Up the Transactors

When users finally decide to sign up, they are brought to a short sign-up page that asks users for the their name, email, and password. By keeping the sign-up short, it stands a better chance of being completed and submitted.

One of the nice touches of this form is that the cursor is automatically placed into the first field. Most users probably won't notice this, but it does make sign-up just a little bit easier. At the top of the right column is a safety link (like a safety net) that redirects existing members to sign in. The right side also includes a reminder that signing up is free (if you don't explicitly tell users that your service is free, they will assume that hidden costs will show up later on) as well as links to member benefits, the quality guarantee, and the privacy policy. All of these items have been selectively included to remove any last-second doubts or concerns. One improvement, however, would be to provide an explanation of how the email address will be used because some users might be spam-a-phobic and choose not to register. At the very least, the privacy policy link could be closer to the email address field.

The sign-up page automatically places the cursor into the first field to make things a little easier.

NOTE   *Spam-a-phobia* is a condition in which Internet users are reluctant to provide true email information for fear of receiving unsolicited email, such as get-rich-quick schemes that allow people to work at home.

Pictures to Go

Right after users sign up, they are directly logged in to the service. Shutterfly's next objective is to get these customers to start using the service, and again, the site provides options for users who are at different stages of readiness.

For users who have digital pictures that they can't wait to get a print of, the site provides a link for users to add their own pictures into the system. For users who currently don't have any pictures to upload, Shutterfly will provide sample photos with which users can try out the service. It's this type of inclusive thinking that enables the site to be able to offer something to all users.

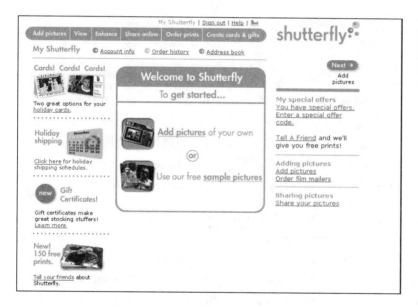

The member home page provides three redundant links (try to find them) to lead users to add their own photos.

When Customers Become Sellers

Shutterfly has a "Tell A Friend" feature that is basically a referral system. Current members can receive free prints for every referred user who signs up. Such referral programs make use of the liking principle in which people tend to be more favorably disposed to a service when a friend recommends it to them.

Shutterfly's referral page places an emphasis on making members comfortable enough to send out the recommendation to their friends.

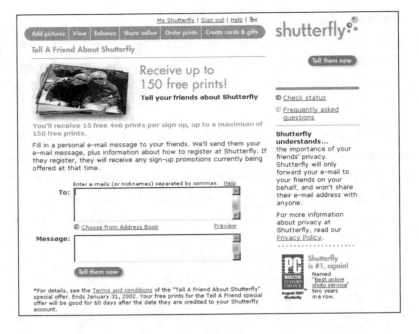

The content on this page is catered to making the referrer comfortable in recommending the service. A summary of the privacy policy is presented to reassure members that their friends' email addresses won't be shared with others. Furthermore, an external award given to the site is highlighted to remind referrers that this is really a good service to recommend to others.

On the receiving end of the referral, the friend will see an email that appears to be from the member. This is done on purpose instead of making Shutterfly the sender because the recipient might arbitrarily delete emails from unknown senders. The email tells the friend that the member will receive free prints if the friend decides to sign up with the service and that the friend will also receive free prints. By creating a win-win situation for both the member and the friend, Shutterfly stands a good chance at winning over more customers.

Booking the Right Trip

Featured Site: Expedia < **www.expedia.com** >

Users

Evaluators   *Transactors*

Expedia is an all-in-one travel site that provides travel booking in five major categories: flights, hotels, cars, vacation packages, and cruises. The goal of this travel site is to help users book as many of these items as possible for a given trip. The challenge with an all-inclusive (forgive the pun) travel site is in catering to both business and leisure travelers simultaneously. Business travelers have more stringent scheduling requirements and are willing to pay a premium for convenience. Leisure travelers are more flexible in their arrangements but are more price sensitive. By being flexible in its design, Expedia is able to cater to the needs of all travelers.

Travel

Searching for Flights

One of the site's main functions is to help users find and select a flight. To this end, Expedia provides many different ways for users to find the flight that best meets their needs.

The Express Search on the home page is the primary means for users to search for flights. If you take a closer look at the search for flights, however, you'll see some of the careful thought that has been put into making it easy for evaluators to decide between travel options.

The Express Search features a drop-down calendar that makes it easy to choose dates.

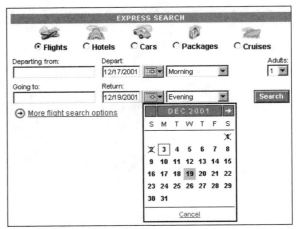

www.expedia.com

Users are first required to specify from where they are departing and to where they are going. These text fields are able to accept city names (such as San Francisco) as inputs as well as airport codes (try to guess which cities are BAH, BUD, and BOG). By being flexible, Expedia makes it easier for users to enter their search criteria.

Next are the date fields. A drop-down calendar is provided to make it easier to select departure and return dates. When the calendar is displayed, the current date is marked, past dates are crossed out, and the selected date is highlighted. The calendar makes it easier for users to book a flight for "next Friday" rather than having to figure out what the date is.

Then there's the time of day. Some airline or travel sites ask users to specify the hour at which they want to depart. The problem with this is that the search might result in no matching flights. Expedia simplifies this by making the time choices more general to increase the likelihood of finding matching flights. Users only have to choose from "Morning," "Noon," or "Evening," and Expedia will search for the flights that best match these time periods.

Something interesting happens, however, when users click the Search button. They are immediately brought to a page that looks like this:

Right after users click the Search button, they are presented with this search-in-progress page so that they don't think that nothing is happening. Notice that the text at the bottom is customized based on the fact that the user is searching for a flight to San Francisco.

This is a search-in-progress page that lets users know that the search is being executed. This type of page should be presented immediately anytime a search or a transaction request will take more than a few seconds to display results or a confirmation. If your users click on a submit button and nothing seems to happen, they will repeatedly click on the button and resubmit their request, compounding the delay in the response. By displaying this in-progress page, users feel like something is happening and are less likely to abandon the site.

Evaluating Flight Options

The search results are very easy to scan. Users can choose to sort results by the lowest price, shortest flights, departure time, or arrival time.

When users select to view the flight details, they are given the option to add a hotel reservation. If users book the hotel, they are also presented with options to add car rentals, cancellation insurance, and even tourist passes in their destination city. This is cross-selling at its best.

At the bottom of the flight details page are all of the booking options. One unique aspect of the calls to action on this page is that they are long and explicit (and no, they're not rap lyrics). Each of the calls to action is a descriptive link so that users know exactly what is going to happen when they click it; this helps users be more confident in clicking on them.

Expedia's booking options allow users to purchase immediately, reserve their seats, or save the flight information for later. This enables users to commit according to their level of readiness to buy.

3 Select a booking option

Fares are not guaranteed until purchased.

→ Review preferences, then purchase. I have read and accept the rules and restrictions.

→ Reserve until midnight tomorrow. I have read and accept the rules and restrictions.

When you reserve, we'll hold your seat until midnight Pacific Time tomorrow. Your fare could go up any time before you pay for this ticket. We recommend you complete your purchase now.

→ Save this information in an itinerary. I have read and accept the rules and restrictions.

Seats are not reserved and fare is not guaranteed.

✕ Cancel and go to home page.

Tickets for Transactors

The process for buying tickets can take many different routes. First-time users are required to fill in their preferences (aisle or window seats, frequent flyer plans, and so on), and the information is stored for later use. Returning users can choose to purchase items using "Express Booking," which automatically uses their default preferences, or they can choose to review and change their preferences before submitting.

Expedia asks its users to provide the last four digits of their credit card number to match it with the one they have on file.

1 Credit card information

We have the following credit card on file.

Card type: Visa
Expiration date: 8/2002

Please provide the last four digits of the credit card number:

Use a different credit card.

For transactors who are concerned about security, the site provides an explanation of secure sockets layer (SSL) encryption. If users are still uncomfortable with providing their credit card number online, they can phone it in and have that credit card stored on file. When users want to make a purchase, they are reminded of the type of credit card on file (Visa, MasterCard, and so on) and its expiration date, and they are asked to enter the last four digits of that credit card to submit the order. By being creative in the way in which it accepts payment method information, Expedia can help more users be comfortable as transactors.

Establishing a Trustworthy Market

Featured Site: eBay < www.ebay.com >

Users

Browsers

Evaluators

Transactors

Customers

Marketplaces are arguably the most compelling online business model because they leverage one of the Internet's strengths in being able to bring together dispersed users to form a community. Marketplaces need to go beyond just connecting buyers with sellers, however; they need to create a trusted environment that facilitates transactions.

eBay is the most well recognized and successful of the online marketplaces. It is an auction site that enables users to post items for sale and solicit bids from potential buyers, with the highest bid winning. With millions of items ranging from Elvis Presley Love Me Tender marbles to Buffy the Vampire Slayer lunch boxes, users can buy and sell virtually anything in this massive, sprawling marketplace.

Marketplace

To be an effective marketplace, eBay must do four things fundamentally well:

1. Help sellers be as effective as possible in selling their products.

2. Help buyers find something of interest.

3. Establish the site as a safe and objective place to conduct transactions.

4. Provide a feedback loop for buyers and sellers to evaluate each other.

As you read through this review of the site, keep these four objectives in mind, and you'll see why eBay is so successful.

Helping Sellers to Sell

eBay is known for the depth of its product selection, but it should also be recognized for the depth of content it provides to help sellers sell.

First, there are narrated tours that walk users through the site. Then, there are recorded seminars that play back recorded versions of live, narrated, online presentations on how to use the site. There are also interactive tutorials that provide step-by-step walk-throughs. There's even an eBay University where new "eBayers" can register for on-site training seminars. eBay has really gone out of its way to provide a complete set of resources to its sellers; the site even provides an HTML tutorial to help sellers enhance the design of their pages. The fact that eBay provides all of these resources says a lot in terms of its determination to help its sellers succeed.

eBay's interactive tutorials help users learn how to sell their items, include photos, and even edit their listings with HTML.

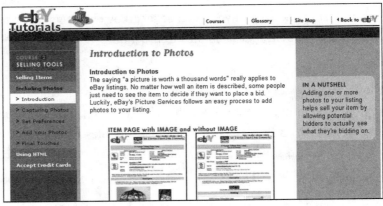

www.ebay.com

So, why does eBay provide all this content and resources? Well, eBay understands that it needs to help its sellers be persuasive. The more effective the sellers are, the higher their selling prices, which results in higher transaction fees for eBay. (Transaction fees are based on a percentage of the selling price.) eBay's resources help sellers learn important tips such as starting out with low minimum bids to attract buyers and that auctions should extend over the weekend because this is when most buyers have time to shop. By providing these resources, eBay helps its sellers create a more compelling marketplace.

Upselling the Sellers

In addition to transaction fees, another source of revenue for eBay is providing product-listing enhancements to sellers. When sellers set up their product listings, they are presented with options such as adding multiple pictures, featuring items in a visual gallery, and highlighting and bolding listing titles for a small fee. Beside each of these options is a link to a corresponding screen shot of how these enhanced features work.

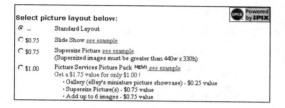

eBay effectively bundles and prices its photo options to persuade sellers to choose the $1.00 Picture Services Picture Pack.

One of the product listing options is to enhance the photo layout. Now, if you've done your homework on the eBay site (aside from reading this book), you'll know that product photos are an important selling point for buyers. Sellers can choose a standard, single-photo layout, or they can opt for more advanced features such as slide shows or supersize pictures. The point of interest, however, is how eBay has priced each of these options. The standard layout is free, and the slide shows or supersize pictures are $0.75 each. But for just $1.00, the seller can choose the Picture Services Picture Pack that includes a supersize picture plus up to six images (or, in other words, "a $1.75 value for only $1.00!"). This is the concept of price anchoring. By setting expectations in terms of what users can get for $0.75, the $1.00 Picture Pack is a persuasive deal by comparison.

Not all enhancements are available to all sellers, however. For example, the Mister Lister service enables sellers to list several items at once, but it is only available to qualified eBay users. To qualify, sellers must have received a minimum amount of positive feedback from their buyers and be registered on eBay for at least 60 days. In this way, eBay encourages its sellers to provide good service to their buyers and prevents poor sellers from being able to add more listings quickly. It's this type of well-crafted rules and regulations that helps eBay maintain the quality of its sellers.

Helping Buyers to Browse

At a simplified level, there are two types of buyers at eBay: those who know what they're looking for and those who don't. Provided that sellers follow the tips for how to label their product listings, buyers who know what they're looking for should be able to find known items using the search. For potential buyers who are just looking around, however, the eBay navigation experience feels very much like a huge garage sale where users just seem to stumble upon items of interest.

When users click on the Browse button in the top navigational bar, they are presented with a long, scrolling page of the main categories and subcategories for product listings. Beside each category heading is a number in brackets that shows off how many items are offered within it. The implicit message behind this page is "We've got a lot of stuff," and it really shows. This is a page built to encourage browsers to explore.

Here's an example of an eBay Browse page showing off just how many items are available at the site.

Consumer Electronics (264560)
Camcorders (4310)
Car Audio & Electronics (18349)
Gadgets & Other Electronics (10804)
Home Audio & Video (34777)
PDAs/Handheld PCs (9645)
Phones & Wireless Devices (49484)
Portable Audio & Video (5188)
Professional Equipment (6309)
Radio Equipment (10439)
Video Games (115273)

In addition to the main Browse page, there are many other ways for users to wander through the site. There are regional pages where users can see items listed within their geographic area, and there are theme-based pages where categories are grouped according to interests (such as fine-art collecting or weddings). Links to various sections of products are even embedded in the help section so that users reading up on shipping tips can see the latest shipping supplies available for sale. It's this type of liberal linking that makes it easy for users to wander around the site.

Motivating Browsers to Bid

One of the challenges for eBay is in helping potential buyers to feel comfortable bidding for a product. This comfort level is addressed through many design features that eBay has included in its product listings.

First, sellers are encouraged to provide thorough, detailed listings with photos of their products. This helps buyers ensure that they've found the right item and that they do in fact want it. Sellers are also encouraged to be explicit regarding the terms of sale so that buyers know exactly how much they are expected to pay up front.

venusrisinglimited 's feedback		Feedback Help | FAQ	
Feedback 1 - 25 of 295			
[1] 2 3 4 5 6 7 8 9 10 11 12 (next page)			
leave feedback for venusrisinglimited	If you are venusrisinglimited : Respond to comments	venusrisinglimited was the **Seller** = S venusrisinglimited was the **Buyer** = B	
Left by	**Date**	**Item#**	**S/B**
iamre@aol.com (100) ⭐	Dec-06-01 09:54:43 PST	1299071286	S
Praise : Another great sheet set. Carefully shipped. Thanks.			
robertpainter (122) ⭐	Dec-04-01 09:05:47 PST	1290962495	S
Praise : Smooth transaction, item as described, fast shipment.			
woodcrestadi@mail.telis.org (837) ⭐	Dec-03-01 08:42:21 PST	1295276226	B
Praise : THANKS FOR ANOTHER SUCCESSFUL EBAY AUTION. GREAT EBAY USER :+)			
chuckytheman (2144) ⭐ me	Nov-29-01 09:41:36 PST	(private)	B
Praise : Fast Payment, Excellent Transaction, Highly Recommended.			
perpetua49@aol.com (192) ⭐	Nov-28-01 13:11:47 PST	1657325022	S
Praise : THE MOST EXQUISITE BEDDING I'VE EVER SEEN!.............Thanks!!!!!!!!!			

Users can see the feedback for particular sellers so that they can determine whether to do business with them.

The second emphasis of the design features is trust. Before buyers can feel comfortable enough to bid, they must have some means of trusting the seller. eBay manages this through its feedback system. In the product listings, the sellers' user IDs have a feedback rating beside them in brackets. (The feedback rating is a cumulative score of all the positive and negative ratings that a user has received.) Clicking on the feedback rating displays whatever feedback this user has received from others. Only users who have actually conducted a transaction with another user can add to the feedback rating. Feedback goes both ways: Buyers can rate sellers and vice versa. Further accountability is provided by the fact that users can see how any user has rated other users. This is a system that encourages users to be honest in their ratings and to be proactive in maintaining a good rating for themselves.

Creating a Safe Place for Transactions

One of eBay's primary strengths is that it is a rich, vibrant online community. Given this context, eBay developers are more than just technologists—they are more like a government. For this marketplace to thrive, eBay has to proactively govern the site and its policies so that commerce can proliferate.

eBay's SafeHarbor area is dedicated to helping users understand what they should do when something goes wrong. This resource area explains all of eBay's policies (for example, listing policies, the tax policy, the system outage policy, and so on) and provides links to all of the services eBay has in place to protect its users from fraud.

eBay's SafeHarbor section provides information about how buyers and sellers are protected on the site.

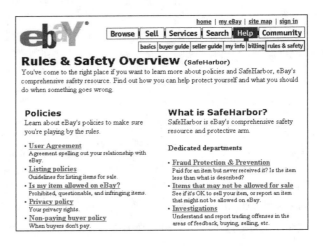

By default, most of eBay's items are covered for up to $200 if buyers purchase items that don't live up to what they expect or if they don't even receive the item. Escrow services are provided so that money can be transferred to sellers via a third party when buyers receive items to their satisfaction. Authentication services are also available to certify the quality and authenticity of collectibles and to verify the identity of individual users. Finally, there is also an online dispute-resolution service managed by SquareTrade that helps users resolve any disputes in their buying or selling.

By going beyond just helping users to find buyers and sellers, eBay is able to create an environment in which users can feel safe doing business.

Attention to Detail Sells

Featured Site: Harrell Remodeling < **www.harrell-remodeling.com** >

Users

Browsers   *Evaluators*

Professional services are about selling expertise and the people behind it. The objective of a professional service site is to convince users that the firm is the right choice to meet their needs. For most of these sites, the primary response is to contact the firm, so these sites are brochures in many cases. There are, however, many little details to be attended to that will make the difference between a user clicking away or deciding to contact the firm. Harrell Remodeling Inc. is one such firm that understands these details.

Harrell Remodeling Inc. provides design and project-management services for remodeling San Francisco Peninsula homes. I know this because it says so on its home page. It's this simple attention to detail that makes this an effective site.

The Harrell Remodeling home page clearly tells users what services the company provides.

www.harrell-remodeling.com

Professional

Pictures That Tell the Story

One of the strengths of this site is its photos. As users click through the Photo Gallery, they are presented with professional photographs of this firm's remodeling work. The quality of the photos helps bring out the quality of their work and provides the most compelling evidence that this is a good firm to hire. One possible way to enhance the photos, however, would be to integrate the actual clients and their testimonials about Harrell Remodeling.

The high-quality photographs of remodeling projects do most of the selling for this site. Notice that the "before" picture is in black and white to provide even greater contrast to the work that was done.

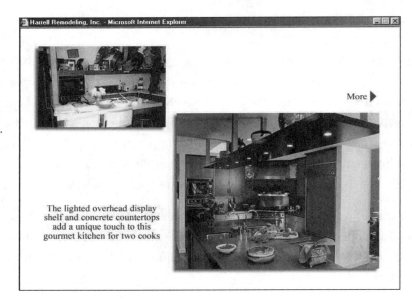

The lighted overhead display shelf and concrete countertops add a unique touch to this gourmet kitchen for two cooks

Selling the People

The quality of the photographs also applies to the About Us section where the members of the management team are featured. Each manager has a professionally shot photo along with a detailed bio. By providing detailed information for each staff member, the firm is able to establish its qualifications. Compare this with the experience of just seeing a list of names that really don't mean anything. By enabling evaluators to get to know the staff a little more, they can become more comfortable with the idea of working with the members of this firm.

Extensive bios help evaluators know the qualifications of Harrell Remodeling's employees.

Helping Evaluators to Be Choosy

My favorite section of this site is called "Choosing a Contractor." What's compelling about this section is that it explains what users should be looking for when hiring a contractor. This helps users to be more knowledgeable about selecting a contractor, and at the same time there is an implicit statement that Harrell Remodeling has all of these qualifications covered.

This information on choosing a contractor advises users to check whether the contractors they are considering are licensed in the state of California and goes so far as to even provide users with a phone number to check.

If you scroll down to the bottom of this section, you'll see a short article called "Getting Ready to Remodel Your Home" that provides some legal tips for dealing with contractors. The persuasive element of this article, however, is the fact that it is written by an attorney who is not part of the remodeling firm. This gives the article more credibility and establishes its objectivity. By paying attention to detail in the content of the web site, Harrell Remodeling establishes its expertise and qualifications as a firm to hire.

Clicking It for Your Web Site

When it comes to designing your own site, you need to determine which types of users are most relevant to supporting your goals. Different types of businesses might validly place a differing emphasis on browsers, evaluators, transactors, and customers. Retail sites might focus more on browsers and evaluators; marketplaces might focus more on customers and so on.

As a closing note for this chapter, remember that what's appropriate and successful on one type of site might seem silly or even counterproductive on another. You have to fall back on an understanding of your users' decision-making process to map out how to design your site.

8

The Persuasive Web Design Process

Now that you've gotten to know each of the users who will visit your site and have learned the most effective ways to put the elements of an effective page together, this chapter will focus on process. There are already many good books on the entire web design and development process, so rather than try to fit a book into a chapter, I will focus on specific design techniques for making sure that your site is persuasively designed. The key to designing persuasive web sites is to seamlessly integrate content with functionality that moves users through their decision-making process.

The following are the essential steps in the persuasive web design process:

- Know the business, user, and web goals for your site.

- Define the content and functionality of the site.

- Choreograph the user experience.

- Conduct persuasion tests.

- Evaluate and improve the site.

The sections that follow walk you through these steps.

Goals, Goals, and More Goals

You hit what you aim for—so the first step toward a successful web site is to define its goals. Well-defined goals provide you with goal posts to evaluate tradeoffs and make design decisions. Defining your goals is a three-step process:

1. Specify your business goals.

2. Identify your users' goals.

3. Merge your business goals and your users' goals to form your web site's goals.

Business Goals

Your business (or organizational) goals are about what you want to accomplish. Here are some examples of goals for different businesses:

Dental Clinic	**Electronics Retailer**	**Bank**
Increase revenue by acquiring more patients.	Increase profitability by selling more high-margin electronics.	Reduce operating costs by encouraging more customers to bank online.

User Goals

At the other end of the spectrum are your users' goals. The fact remains that it's the users who are navigating through your site, so you must design with their goals in mind. If you don't help your users meet their goals, they will simply find another site that will. The quick way to define user goals is to interview users and ask them to express what their goals are as it pertains to your products and services. Here are some sample user goals based on the businesses mentioned previously:

Dental Patient	**Electronics Purchaser**	**Bank Customer**
I want a reputable dental clinic that will meet all of my family's dental needs.	*Find me a high-quality home theater setup at a reasonable price.*	*Make my banking more convenient.*

Web Site Goals

When you compare business goals and user goals, you'll usually see that there are some overlaps and some gaps. Your web site sits between your business and your users, and it needs to strengthen the commonalities between goals while bridging any gaps between them. In other words, your web site needs to support users' attempts to accomplish their goals in order to drive them to meet your business's goals.

To be effective, web site goal statements must do the following:

- **Be persuasive.** Web site goals must recognize that users are in control and that they need to be guided and supported to transact. Words like "persuade," "motivate," and "support" should be used in your web site goals to remind you that you need to earn your users' business.

- **Specify an audience.** Your web site can't please absolutely everyone, so you need to design it with a specific audience in mind. Different types of users have different criteria (consider a college student looking for a bookshelf stereo versus an audiophile purchasing a home theater system), so it's important to specify a target audience for each web site goal.

- **Specify a desired response.** All web site goals must clearly specify how users should respond. For each site goal, you might have a primary response as the preferred user response and secondary responses as a fallback. The purpose of defining primary and secondary responses is to determine the priority in which calls to action should be presented onscreen. (For example, primary responses should be more prominent and repeatedly displayed.) Keep in mind, however, that responses do not have to occur online—it's perfectly fine for a response to be realized in another channel.

Here are some examples of site goals for the three businesses we've been using:

Dental Clinic	Electronics Retailer	Bank
Site Goal To convince families that this is a reputable and professional clinic that can competently meet all of their dental needs.	**Site Goal** To support audiophiles in being able to select the best and most profitable home theater systems that meet their budget constraints.	**Site Goal** To persuade current bank customers that online banking is a safe, secure, and convenient way to do their banking.
Primary Response ■ Call the clinic to schedule an appointment.	**Primary Response** ■ Purchase a high-margin home theater system online.	**Primary Response** ■ Sign up for online banking.
Secondary Response ■ Email the clinic to schedule an appointment. ■ Call or email the clinic to request more information.	**Secondary Response** ■ Purchase a home theater system online. ■ Register to become a member of the site to store account information.	**Secondary Response** ■ Persuade new customers to open a bank account.

As you review each of these sample goals, you'll notice that there is a sequential priority in terms of the preferred responses from users. (Note that there is only one primary response for each.) These priorities will help you design and lay out your site so that the call to actions are appropriately emphasized. (You'll read more about how to prioritize a bit later.)

Defining Content and Functionality

The next step in the process is to define your site's content and functionality. Provided that your site is fundamentally usable, it will be your site's content and functionality that will determine how persuasive it is. You need to develop the right content to educate and inform your users and couple it with the right functionality that will help users make a decision.

A good way to get started in determining your site's content and functionality is to use the browser-evaluator-transactor-customer framework you learned about in Chapters 2 through 5. By looking at your site and its goals from the perspective of these four user types, you can quickly come up with a list of content and functionality. Here's a checklist of questions to ask yourself to define or evaluate your own site:

Browsers

- Is it clear where users should start navigating to accomplish their goals?
- Can users tell what your site offers? Do they perceive your whole range of products and services?
- Do you make it easy for users to navigate through related content, products, or services? How do you encourage users to wander around your site?
- What educational material do your provide to help your users become confident evaluators?
- Is it immediately obvious to your users why they need your products or services? If not, how do you intend to make them aware?
- Does the site stimulate users to recognize unrealized needs?

Evaluators

- How will you enable your users to quickly evaluate between options?
- How do you prove that your product or service is worth purchasing? Do you provide enough detail for users to want it?
- Does your content explain the features and benefits of your products and services?
- Are the right photos or images incorporated in your content to show off your products and services in the best possible light?
- Do you provide design tools or calculators to help users determine their own specific solution?
- Do you allow users to get a real sense of how your product or service works? Do you need to provide a demo?

Transactors

- Do you make it easy for your users to transact at any time throughout the site?
- Do you allow your users to continue with a transaction that they previously started?
- How do you support users that already know what they want?
- Do you specify any requirements that users have to fulfill up front before they start the transaction?
- Do you provide guarantees or assurances to help users overcome any hesitancy regarding transacting online?
- How do you motivate your users to complete their transaction immediately? What sorts of incentives or disincentives do you incorporate?

Customers

- How do you intend to draw your customers back to your site?
- How do you enable customers to solve their own problems or answer their own questions?
- How do you enable customers to vent and receive a quick resolution to their problems?
- How do you make it easier for customers to conduct the next transaction?
- What incentives do you provide customers to do business with you again?

Learning from Your Users

The browser-evaluator-transactor-customer framework is a good starting point for identifying site content and functionality, but it's no substitute for learning directly from your users. They are the ones who need to be convinced to transact, and the more you know what is important to them, the better you will be able to deliver site content and functionality that will get them to transact. Here are some techniques for learning from your users:

- **Interview your users.** You need to ask your target audience two fundamental questions:

  1. What features and benefits are most important to you about these products or services?

  2. What problems or negative consequences do you want to avoid with these products or services?

     These questions are based on the fundamental elements of persuasion: the desire for reward and the fear of punishment. Here's a third, follow-up question that you should use:

  3. What would it take to get you to purchase this product or service right now?

     This last question is about learning how you can motivate your users to transact.

- **Observe your users performing similar tasks offline.** In Paco Underhill's book *Why We Buy: The Science of Shopping* (2000, Touchstone, New York), he talks about teams of shopping "trackers" who spend countless hours watching how shoppers shop. They observe how people walk through stores, the signs they notice, and how they examine items before making a purchase. This is about observing people in real life and learning what they do instead of just what they say they do.

If applicable, try to observe people as they decide whether to purchase your products or services in the real world. If you sell clothing, you should observe people in clothing stores; if you sell professional services, sit in on a sales presentation; if you sell financial services, listen in as a customer talks to a bank representative about getting a loan. Note the types of questions they ask, how they evaluate the product or service, and any concerns or doubts that arise. Just watch, listen, and learn.

- **Interview the people who interact with your users.** If you don't have much time, an alternative (although less than ideal) to talking with or observing users directly is to speak to the people who come in regular contact with them. Talk to salespeople or customer service representatives and ask them for the same type of information you would have gathered via user interview or observation.

- **Lurk in newsgroups.** Newsgroups are online discussion forums that enable users to post questions and receive responses from group participants. Many people use newsgroups as a starting point for investigating their purchases and soliciting consumer feedback.

    When you go to a newsgroup site such as Google groups < groups.google.com >, you can do a search for the products or services you offer to see what people are saying about them. Newsgroups are often a venting ground, and they provide an excellent source of ideas for improving your site and identifying the issues that are important to your users.

    When scanning through newsgroups, take special note of how users phrase their concerns. You can use these exact phrases in your content so that your users will immediately identify with the words used. In fact, I know of one large software company that developed its banner ads based on quotes gathered from newsgroups; this better reflects the voice of the customer.

Prioritizing Goals, Content, and Functionality

One of the common challenges in any project is to prioritize competing web site goals to allocate resources to develop content and functionality. The scenario usually starts with prioritizing items as Low, Medium, or High. Inevitably what happens is that the majority of goals are labeled High, so you end up creating new levels of highness such as Very High or Super High. One effective means of getting around this is to bring in the main stakeholders and have them each divide $100 between the various items. This helps people critically evaluate the relative priority between competing items, and it prevents every item from being a high priority.

Content: Introduction to home theater systems	Content: How to set up your home theater system	Function: Home theater comparison tool	Content: Home theater recommender for different budgets	Content: Multiple product photos for each product	Content: Detailed specs for each product
$15.00	$10.00	$15.00	$30.00	$5.00	$25.00

By dividing $100 dollars into your proposed content and functionality, you can quickly reach a consensus regarding priorities and can understand the relative importance of each item. This same exercise can be used for prioritizing goals.

When you go through the exercise of allocating the $100, you should keep the following in mind:

- **Prioritize items that support the decision process.** If it doesn't bring your users closer to transacting, get rid of it.

- **Listen to what your users tell you.** Prioritize items based on what users have told you during their interviews and what you've observed them doing during their decision-making process.

- **Leave the bells and whistles for last.** Most users aren't interested in fancy tools unless they help them decide in some way.

- **Consider complexity and impact.** Prioritize the items that are easy to implement but yield a great impact (otherwise known as "low-hanging fruit").

Choreographing the Experience

After you've decided on your site's content and functionality, you need to string these elements together to create a choreographed user experience. It's like movie-making: You spend time up front drafting and iterating ideas to get an understanding of how things should flow before committing to film or, in the case of the web, to HTML.

In figuring out how to choreograph content and functional elements together, I find that employing a three-pronged combination of use-case scenarios, navigation maps, and wireframes is an effective design process. Each of these processes is a different way of describing the user experience, and they help you to rethink the experience by forcing you to adopt different perspectives. As a result, your user experience will be much more robust and well thought-out from the beginning rather than finding missing gaps or inconsistencies as you're developing the site (or even after it's launched!).

Let's examine these three processes through the example of someone registering to become a member of an online service such as designing and ordering stationery online.

Use-Case Scenarios

This process uses words to describe a flow of events. Use-case scenarios are a step-by-step script describing what users do and how the system responds to their actions.

The following is a simplified, practical format that I have found to be effective for describing use-case scenarios. There are many different methods for describing use cases, but I've found this format to be an easy and clear method.

The first component is called the *normal case*, in which the user's actions and system responses are going according to the desired route. To provide some context, I also have included the business, user, and web site goals.

Goals	
Business goal	To get as many users as possible to begin using the service and generating revenue.
User goal	To find a reliable, secure, and efficient means to design and order business stationery.
Web site goal	To persuade small business owners to begin using the service and make it easy for them to register within five minutes without assistance.

Normal Case

Step	User Action	System Response
1.0	The user selects the option to find out more about the service.	The system presents content explaining the service as well as customer testimonials describing on how reliable, secure, and efficient it is to use the service.
2.0	The user selects the option to register and become a member of the service.	The system asks users to enter the following information: ■ Name ■ Email address ■ User ID ■ Password
3.0	The user enters all required information correctly.	The system displays the user's entered information for confirmation and presents users with the option to cancel the registration, modify the entered information, or submit the information for registration.
4.0	The user selects the option to submit the information.	The system confirms to the user that the registration information has been submitted and logs them in to the customer site.

Based on the preceding example, however, there are variations in terms of how the scenario could flow. Variations capture different paths that the user could choose to click through and are referred to as variation cases (brilliant, huh?). A variation in the preceding scenario might be that the user chooses to go back to modify the information instead of submitting it. Normal cases describe the intended, optimal flow of the scenario, and variation cases capture anticipated deviations. Each step in the normal case can have multiple variations, as shown in the following example:

Variation Cases

Step	User Action	System Response
4.1	The user selects the option to cancel the registration.	The system displays that the registration is cancelled and that no information has been submitted.
4.2	The user selects the option to modify the information.	The system returns user to step 1.0 but with the capability to modify the information that already has been entered.

Steps 4.1 and 4.2 represent two separate variations of step 4.0. If step 4.1 had multiple steps behind it, you could label these steps as 4.10, 4.11, 4.12, and so on.

The final type of use-case scenario is *error cases*. These cases cover when things go wrong. More often than not, most designers and developers focus on building the functionality for the normal case and then deal with error handling at the end. The assumption is that users will figure out how the interaction is supposed to work and will make no mistakes.

Let's not make the mistake of assuming that all users will get it right the first time—you have to be proactive in designing for error situations to ensure a higher success rate for your users. The last thing you want is for motivated users to leave in frustration because the error handling was poorly implemented due to a last-minute hack. Error handling needs to be thought about and incorporated at the outset to ensure that it is planned for in the scope of development.

The error cases cover all of the errors that might occur either in the normal case or in the variation cases.

Error Cases

Step	User Action	System Response
3.0a	The user does not enter all of the required information.	The system displays that an error has occurred and identifies which additional information needs to be entered.
3.0b	The user does not enter the information correctly.	The system displays that an error has occurred, identifies which information has been incorrectly input, and provides guidance as to how to correct the information entered.

Steps 3.0a and 3.0b are separate error variations of step 3.0. If there are multiple steps behind recovering from a particular error such as 3.0a, the steps can be recorded as 3.0a1, 3.0a2, and so on.

Use-case scenarios are a very useful (pardon the pun) way of imagining how the interaction between the user and system should work. It's important, however, for these use-case scenarios to be written in a specific manner; otherwise, they can compromise your site's design. Here are some tips to keep in mind as you develop and work with use-case scenarios:

- **They should not contain any design details.** Use-case scenarios need to stick to describing the interaction and avoid mentioning any design specifics. If your scenarios specify that users click the Submit button or click the drop-down menu to make a selection, they are too specific. By describing only the essential interaction, you will be better able to maintain an open mind toward how the scenario could be designed and implemented. For example, in the error cases mentioned, the final design could be met through presenting separate error web pages or through JavaScript pop-ups. The point is that you shouldn't specify either at this point to avoid boxing in the design too early.

- **Capture all variations and errors up front.** Use-case scenarios are used to understand the full scope of what needs to be delivered up front. Take the time to brainstorm and think through all the variations at the outset to avoid discovering additional "must-have" requirements at the end.

- **Capture future functionality as change cases.** After you've identified all of the possible variations and errors, you will probably discover that you can't implement them all. What you might do then is change your use cases so that their requirements are easier to implement. You should, however, keep track of any ideas that you didn't implement as change cases—this can help you make sure you don't lose any great ideas for use in the future. The reality, however, is that anything to be addressed in some future release often doesn't happen. Don't be too liberal in just labeling anything as a change case because it stands a good chance of being ignored. The best time to develop the appropriate solution is the first time because it is often difficult to revisit existing functionality.

- **Don't forget nonfunctional requirements.** The scenarios just described don't paint a complete picture of the design requirements. Although they are a great way of describing the intended interaction, they don't make any reference to the "soft" side of requirements. Users are humans (at least the ones I know), and they have feelings and emotional needs that need to be met. I'm not talking about late-night online chat rooms, but I am referring to addressing users' security concerns and other motivating elements that might either deter or encourage users to transact. You must constantly ask yourself, "Why should the user take this action?" and "What would prevent him from actually completing it?" and incorporate the answers as requirements.

Navigation Maps

The second viewpoint to describe the user experience is through navigation maps. These are diagrams that provide a visual representation of the flow between different screens presented to the user. Navigation maps can be drawn with any software tool, but I have personally found Visio to be the product best suited the task, given the way it enables you to easily make template diagram elements.

Currently, there's no standard nomenclature for diagramming navigation maps. You can, however, borrow from software diagramming conventions so that it is easier for more people to understand. Before you diagram the registration example covered in the use-case scenarios, here's a rundown of the main diagram elements you'll need to know:

Page

The fundamental building block of any web site is a page, and this is represented by a simple rectangle. The page name in the middle of the rectangle should be the page title as it is intended to appear in the actual presented page. A page in this context means a single page of presentation that might be made up of one or more HTML pages (as in a frameset).

Connector

Lines that connect pages or any other navigation map elements are called connectors. Connectors represent paths or links that the user might use to move through the experience. Arrowheads indicate the directional flow between elements, and labels can be added to represent the button label or link that the connector represents.

Page Component

A page component is represented by a rectangle with rounded corners. Page components aren't separate pages, but they represent visual or logical groupings of links or functions that appear on a page. For example, a search field text box on a home page could be described as a page component: It is a separate logical area but is not a distinct separate page.

Linked Page

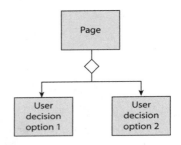

A linked page uses the same rectangle as a page except that
it's dotted. Linked pages connect you to a page that resides
in another section of the site. (For you Star Trek fans, this would be the
equivalent of a worm hole.) The linked page representation prevents you
from having to draw a circular navigation map that links back to itself over
and over again.

User Decision

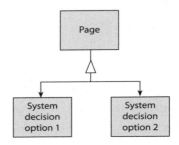

A diamond represents a user decision. User
decisions are the choices that a user might
select within a particular component of functionality. It's important not to confuse user
decisions with links. User decisions are variations within a specific function (like a registration or a shopping cart), whereas links represent connections to
other pages.

System Decision

A system decision is represented by a triangle.
System decisions present the various paths
that users are routed down depending on the
inputs they provide. In other words, the system decides where users go based on what
they submit.

NOTE   For a more exhaustive reference on navigation map diagrams that comple-
ments what has been presented in this section, go to **www.jjg.net/ia**.

Now that you know what the diagram elements look like, here is what a
navigation map would look like for the registration use-case scenario:

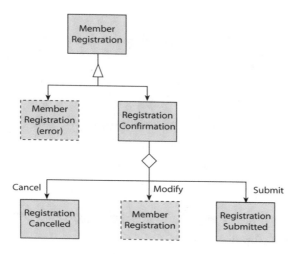

Here are some tips to consider when drawing and using your navigation maps:

- **Don't be cheap with the paper.** When I first began drawing navigation map diagrams, I had one goal in mind: to cram the diagram onto one sheet of paper. Although this has a practical intention, the compromise is that you end up with an unusable and crowded diagram. Navigation maps should be as big as they need to be so that they are clear and easy to understand.

- **Have one overall site navigation map and several smaller ones.** If your site map is starting to get too big, you might consider having an overall navigation map coupled with more detailed navigation maps for logical groups or functions. Although maintaining one gigantic map might help provide a complete picture, you'll find that it's more difficult to maintain, and you'll soon tire of repeatedly taping together tiles of paper.

- **Compare the navigation maps for similar sections.** Navigation maps are useful for maintaining consistency between the interactive elements of your site. As you diagram similar functions across the site, you should double-check that the way the screens connect and flow into one another is consistent. For example, for the registration scenario, you could compare its navigation map with other similar functions to ensure that they have the same confirmation and error-handling scheme.

Wireframes

The third way to describe the user experience is through wireframes. These are black and white sketches or drawings that represent the screens users will see on the site. They are called wireframes because they provide only an outline sketch as to what the web pages will look like. Wireframes are analogous to storyboards in the movie industry. Wireframes should not be graphically designed because their purpose is to provide a quick way to design, evaluate, and iterate the way in which your site content and functionality should be laid out.

Here are a few simple examples of wireframe pages that could be used to illustrate the registration scenario.

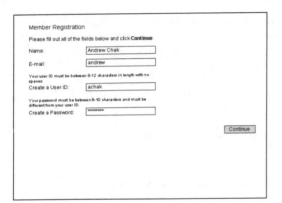

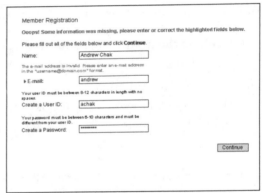

Wireframes should be simple sketches that you can quickly revise and not get attached to. If you're starting to incorporate drop shadows and beveled edges, you're probably going too far.

When it comes to designing pages, there is often the temptation to go straight into graphic-designed mockups (that is, by using imaging programs such as Photoshop) or even into HTML. The point of wireframes is to help you focus on the content and interaction of a page rather than getting caught up in design details such as fonts, colors, and your favorite rollover. Another advantage with wireframes is that they look "rough" enough for people to provide honest feedback about them—it's much harder to be critical of a beautifully rendered layout.

For most people (for example, the rest of your team members), wireframes are easier to understand than use-case scenarios and navigation maps. Although you could use any drawing tool to create wireframes (or you could even hand draw them), I usually make them in a presentation program such as PowerPoint because it enables me to distribute an electronic file that recipients can click through to see the sequence of screens for a given scenario. The essence of the process is not to focus on any given program, however, but to focus on quickly sketching out what the screen elements look like.

Persuasion Testing

After you've designed your screens, the next step is to test them. Usability tests are usually task oriented. For example, an e-commerce usability test might ask users to "Find the first book written by John Grisham and purchase it." The test moderator would observe users as they completed this task and would make a note of any difficulties. These observations, along with the users' feedback, would be used to make design changes, and ideally, the interface would be tested and revised through multiple iterations. This is fine, assuming you have customers who are into John Grisham novels and are motivated to buy on your site. The problem with usability tests, however, is that they test a specific task, and they assume that a user wants to do that task.

Persuasion testing takes usability tests one step further by observing the overall effectiveness of the site and evaluating how well it influences users to transact. Persuasion tests are really variants of usability tests, and there are three types of tests you can conduct: goal-oriented tests, site-level comparisons, and product-selection tests.

Goal-Oriented Tests

This first type of persuasion test evaluates how well a site supports users in accomplishing their goals. The results of this test will give you an indication of the type of content and functionality your site needs in order to support your users through their decision process.

One important aspect of a goal-oriented test is that you need to recruit users who are in the mindset of purchasing the product or service you offer, as opposed to recruiting users who belong to a particular demographic. If you operate a travel site, you would look for people who are looking to buy a vacation package. These users would be brought in, and you (as the moderator) would ask them to use the site to look for a vacation. You would ask these users to speak out loud any thoughts going through their head, observe them using the interface, and take notes.

Find a vacation that meets your needs.

Goal-oriented tests evaluate how well a web site supports users' goals and leads them to a call to action.

The benefit of a goal-oriented test is that it doesn't restrict users to a particular task. With the travel site example, you aren't asking users to find a five-star resort in Cancun and book it for the week of February 2. Instead, you're asking them to use the site to accomplish their goal of finding a vacation. You just sit back and watch them navigate (but make sure you take notes!) and use the site however they want.

When you tell users to perform a specific task, you are making an assumption that they would normally want to do that task. By leaving the test open-ended, you get a glimpse of how people are thinking through the problem and how they would approach using your site. Another main benefit of this test is that it enables you to see the "natural paths" that users tend to take in using your site so that you can take advantage of them in iterating your site design. An important drawback, however, is that you'll need a greater number of test participants to get a sense of the patterns and to make sure you've found the important issues.

Site-Level Comparisons

The best way to evaluate a site's persuasiveness is by comparison. If you were to ask people to use a site and then ask them, "Would you do business with this site?" a lot of users would probably respond positively. The problem is that what people say is often not what they do, and for the sake of being polite, people would be more inclined to say "yes" when they don't really mean it.

A site-level comparison involves putting two sites side by side. Let's say that Site A is your site and Site B is a competitor's. You would recruit users as you did for the goal-oriented test, but you would ask them to use one site and provide feedback and then use the other site and provide feedback. To make the test fair, you would ask half of your users to use Site A first and the other half to use Site B first. At the end of the session, you would ask them which of the two sites they would prefer to do business with and why. Comparing the two sites makes it easier for users to articulate the features that they do and don't like about your site.

Which of these two web sites would you prefer to do business with and why?

Site-level comparisons help users identify what they like and don't like about your site.

The results of this test give you an overall impression of how safe and secure users feel about using your site as compared to others, and they also provide additional insights regarding your site's content and functionality. Another variant of this test is to use your current site and test it against a prototype of a revised version of your site.

Product-Selection Tests

This third test is the most granular and detailed because it is about evaluating individual content pages. Think of it as the Pepsi taste challenge for web pages in which you ask users to separately review two or more different product pages and them ask them to choose which product they would select and why. The purpose here is to evaluate the effectiveness of the specific wording and content of the product descriptions to see what users respond to positively.

Which of these products would you buy?

Product-selection tests help you identify which product features and descriptions work with users.

Another variation of this test is to evaluate different versions of your product descriptions. One version could feature short bullet-point descriptions, and the other could feature long paragraphs of detail. (Some products sell better with lots of details.) You could even test two sets of descriptions for the same product to see which one is more effective.

The feedback you receive from this test will help you refine these product or services pages. Getting these pages right will help you sell much more effectively.

Evaluating and Improving Your Site

As time goes by and you start staring at your site, the inevitable itch occurs—the itch for a redesign. For whatever reason, designers tend to have this compelling urge to want to change things. If they could, they would redesign their sites over and over again with the assumption that each change would be an improvement. Change isn't always good, however, and on the web it might even alienate some of your existing users.

Redesigns don't have to mean big changes—little changes can mean a lot. Quicken added a yellow box to highlight one of its key functions, and its usage rates skyrocketed. Such usability improvements will continue to be a priority to support those motivated users who want to transact.

The small yellow box on the left side of the Quicken Loans home page has resulted in more users checking up on their loan status. Big improvements don't have to come from big changes.

www.quicken.com

As you evolve your site, don't focus on the bells and whistles. Don't add more functionality to your site unless your users ask for it or you notice that they're not following through on their transactions. Do focus on making their decision process easier and easier. This way, you can capitalize on the next phase of growth for sites as they become more persuasive in convincing even unmotivated users to transact.

A Final Word

Thanks for spending time with me as you made your way through *Submit Now: Designing Persuasive Web Sites*. I hope you've found this book to be stuffed with real-world examples, good insights, practical suggestions, and lots of thought-provoking ideas about who customers are, what they want, and how you can best provide it. My hope is that this book has helped you look at your web site in a new way so that you can evaluate design, content, and functionality ideas in the context of achieving your goals. By focusing your site on moving users through the decision-making process, you can better your chances of turning them from visitors to customers. Ultimately, people come to web sites because they're curious, but they stick around because something works for them. As designers, it's up to us to continue to care and learn about what customers want and to keep finding new and better ways to keep them coming back.

Resources

The following books and web sites have helped to open my mind to understanding how we can influence others to do what we want them to do. The books provide more of a perspective about users and how to design for them, while the web sites cover specific areas of web design that are required to create a persuasive experience.

Books

The following books have both influenced and persuaded me (sorry, bad pun) on how to better think about and design web sites. They aren't all directly about web design, but they will challenge you to think from your users' perspective to help them to transact.

Customer Centered Selling

Robert L. Jolles, Fireside, 1998.

This book teaches you how to effectively sell to customers by focusing on their needs. By walking through the customer-decision cycle, you will better understand how prospects need to be guided through the steps they take to make a purchase.

Customer-Effective Web Sites

Jodie Dalgleish, Prentice Hall PTR, 2000.

This is a book for those of us who live by process. It covers an end-to-end process that ensures that the customer is the focal point for all design decisions. Topics such as customer-effective testing, setting up the project team, and e-service requirements definitions make this a useful read for web designers, project managers, and e-commerce business managers alike.

Customers.com

Patricia B. Seybold, Random House, 1998.

This is perhaps considered the original book about adopting the customer perspective on the Internet. The emphasis here is on making it easy for your customers to do business with you. Although it's a little dated now, I still find the principles to be relevant, and I especially enjoy reading the war stories through the many case studies presented in the book.

Don't Make Me Think

Steve Krug, New Riders Publishing, 2000.

This is *the* primer for the essentials of web usability. It's short and fun to read and is the best book to convince yourself and your manager about the value of making your site easy to use. This book helps you understand that users don't want to think when they use your web site; they just want to get their tasks done.

E-Service: 24 Ways to Keep Your Customers When the Competition Is Just a Click Away

Ron Zemke and Tom Connellan, AMACOM, 2000.

This book provides a good overview about customer service on the Internet. Interesting insights are presented on what customer loyalty really means and why keeping customers is more important than acquiring them.

Influence: The Psychology of Persuasion

Robert B. Cialdini, William Morrow & Company, Inc., 1993.

This is one of the most influential books on how to persuade people. By understanding the mental shortcuts people use in making decisions, you can be much more effective at getting people to comply without exerting force. This is a must-read to understand the psychological secrets behind effective persuasion.

Web Navigation: Designing the User Experience

Jennifer Fleming, O'Reilly & Associates, Inc., 1998.

This is one of the earliest books about web design that got it right. The book focuses on designing navigational experiences that remove barriers so that users can get to what they want. Case studies and interviews with leading designers make this a good read on how you should think about and design your site's navigation.

Why We Buy: The Science of Shopping

Paco Underhill, Touchstone, 2000.

Although this is a book about clicks and mortar retailing, it's an enjoyable read that will give you new insights as to how people shop in the offline world. You'll read about interesting tidbits such as the "butt-brush factor" and the "boomerang effect" that will change the way you look at shopping.

Web Sites

If you have a desire to learn more about how to make your site more effective and persuasive, then get comfortable in front of your computer, open up your browser, and type in the following URLs. These are the bookmarks I've referred to on an ongoing basis to develop this book, and now they are yours as well.

Persuasion

Captology: Computers as Persuasive Technologies   www.captology.com

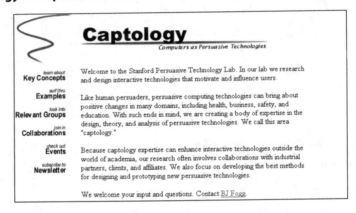

"Captology" is a term coined by the Stanford Persuasive Technology Lab to describe interactive technologies that motivate and influence users. Key concepts are elaborated through topic papers such as "Elements of Computer Credibility" and "Seductive Computing." Make sure you also take a look at the Web Credibility Project site < www.webcredibility.org >, which is dedicated to understanding what makes people trust web sites.

Converting Web Site Traffic   www.clickz.com/sales/traffic

Bryan Eisenberg writes this weekly column that appears as part of the Clickz Network. Although this isn't a persuasion site per se, this column provides a lot of useful tips for converting browsers to customers. Going beyond usability is the mantra here, as you learn how to persuade, guide, and support users to transact. You should also take a look at other Clickz columns such as "Connecting with the Consumer," "Email Marketing," and "Writing Online."

Information Architecture

Argus Center for Information Architecture

If there ever were an official site for information architecture, the Argus Center for Information Architecture would be it. Peter Morville and Louis Rosenfeld, authors of *Information Architecture for the World Wide Web* (also known as the polar bear book), are the site's main custodians. The site is well organized (of course), and the main section to check out is the "ia guide" that enables you to navigate topics by expert picks, author, title, and subject. The "More by Argus" section also includes some good articles and original white papers discussing information architecture.

iaslash   www.iaslash.org

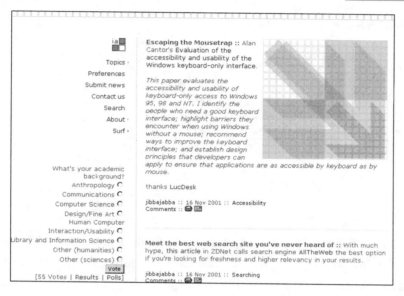

Michael Angeles maintains this web log, where he posts links and excerpts of information architecture–related articles. There are usually a handful of posts each day, and they are categorized so you can review related postings. Some interesting topics include the "Top 10 Stories" (which showcases the most popular postings), the "Site Critiques" area (which features expert reviews of other sites), and the "Industry" topic (which has links to articles about how information architecture is evolving). I usually refer to this site in combination with WebWord (see the following Usability section) to get my daily dose of the latest in user-experience news, articles, and resources.

Usability

Usable Web

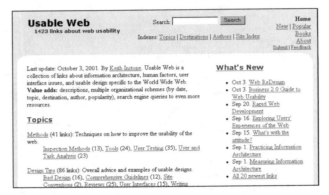

This site is basically the Yahoo! of usability. Keith Instone maintains this site in a directory format, and you can view usability links by date, topic, destination, author, and popularity. It's a great starting point for locating the available resources for a given usability topic.

WebWord.com

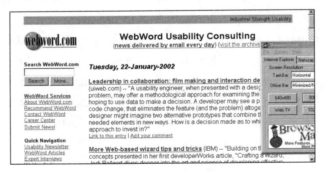

This usability web log by John S. Rhodes compiles the latest usability information available on the Net. This site goes beyond being just a collection of links by featuring original articles, research, and even interviews with user-experience pundits from all over the web. What makes this site an interesting read is John's color commentary on the postings; it makes you feel more like you're watching a sportscast. I especially recommend that you subscribe to the email version to make sure you get all the latest and greatest.

CHI-Web Archive

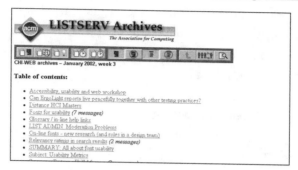

If you've got a usability question, the CHI-Web Archive might provide the answer. CHI stands for Computer Human Interaction, and this is an email discussion group in which many usability practitioners and gurus participate. Questions such as *"Should I label my form buttons as Save or Submit?"* and *"How do I convince upper management on the value of user experience?"* are answered, argued, and debated. To subscribe to this mailing list, send an email to **listserv@acm.org** with the body of your email containing just "subscribe chi-web."

Usability InfoCentre

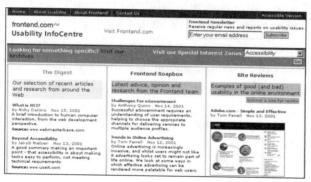

The Usability InfoCentre is run by an Irish usability engineering firm called Frontend. The first main section is the "Digest," where you'll find selected links to recent articles and research on the web. Next comes the "Frontend Soapbox," where members from the firm publish original articles on usability advice, opinion, and research. Finally, my favorite section is "Site Reviews," where they provide positive and negative feedback on both North American and European sites. I make it a point to visit this site every so often to expose myself to other usability perspectives that might not be prevalent in a North American context.

Software Usability Research Laboratory   psychology.wichita.edu/surl/Index.html

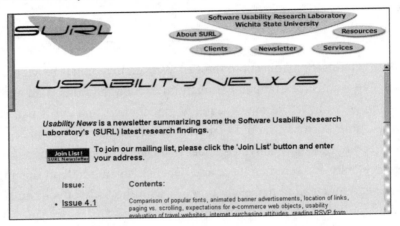

The Software Usability Research Laboratory (SURL) is affiliated with Wichita State University. This site features a newsletter called "Usability News" that summarizes the group's latest usability research findings. Useful topics such as banner blindness and where users expect to see common e-commerce objects (for example, shopping carts) are covered and are based on their original research.

Retail

Internet Retailer

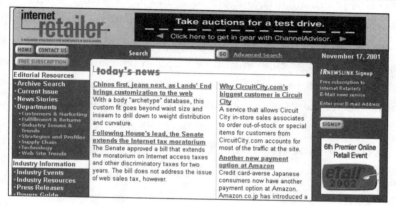

This is a companion site to *Internet Retailer Magazine*, but it is also a searchable archive of staff-written news features and Internet retailing–related press releases. Topics covered include web-based merchandising, multichannel integration, supply-chain automation, and corporate management. This is a good place to check out the competition and to get some new ideas for making your retail site more effective.

Internet Statistics

Nua.com

If you need some up-to-the-minute statistics to help inform your design decisions or you want to find out the latest Internet trends, head on over to the Nua site. Information is categorized according to sectors (such as customer service, e-commerce, and travel), society (such as communities, privacy, and security issues), tools (such as browsers and security tools), and demographics (such as children, women, and usage patterns). Go to this site to find the latest interesting tidbit on why web users won't pay for content or the secret habits of how online moms use the Internet.

And If You've Got the Time...

Orisinal   www.orisinal.com

If you need a break from all of this persuasion and usability (I sure do!), click your browser over to Orisinal. This site is a collection of some of the best and most original Flash-based games on the Internet developed by Ferry Halim. I've spent countless hours here playing some of my favorites games such as "The Amazing Dare Dozen," "Chicken Wing," and "Bum Bum Koala." Trust me, it's worth the visit.

Index

Solutions from experts you know and trust.

www.informit.com

OPERATING SYSTEMS

WEB DEVELOPMENT

PROGRAMMING

NETWORKING

CERTIFICATION

AND MORE...

Expert Access.
Free Content.

New Riders has partnered with **InformIT.com** to bring technical information to your desktop. Drawing on New Riders authors and reviewers to provide additional information on topics you're interested in, **InformIT.com** has free, in-depth information you won't find anywhere else.

- **Master the skills you need, when you need them**

- **Call on resources from some of the best minds in the industry**

- **Get answers when you need them, using InformIT's comprehensive library or live experts online**

- **Go above and beyond what you find in New Riders books, extending your knowledge**

As an **InformIT** partner, **New Riders** has shared the wisdom and knowledge of our authors with you online. Visit **InformIT.com** to see what you're missing.

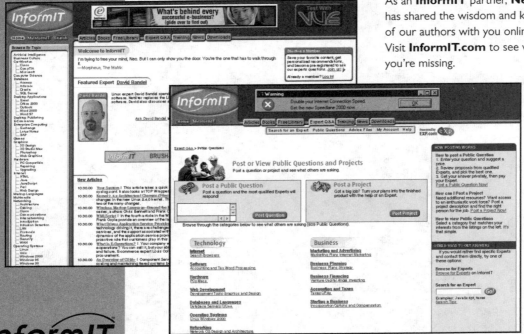

www.informit.com ▪ www.newriders.com

Publishing
the Voices
that Matter

OUR AUTHORS

PRESS ROOM

web development | design | photoshop | new media | 3-D | server technologies

EDUCATORS

ABOUT US

CONTACT US

You already know that New Riders brings you the **Voices that Matter**.

But what does that mean? It means that New Riders brings you the

Voices that challenge your assumptions, take your talents to the next

level, or simply help you better understand the complex technical world

we're all navigating.

Visit **www.newriders.com** to find:

- ▸ 10% discount and free shipping on all purchases
- ▸ Never before published chapters
- ▸ Sample chapters and excerpts
- ▸ Author bios and interviews
- ▸ Contests and enter-to-wins
- ▸ Up-to-date industry event information
- ▸ Book reviews
- ▸ Special offers from our friends and partners
- ▸ Info on how to join our User Group program
- ▸ Ways to have your Voice heard

New
Riders

WWW.NEWRIDERS.COM

VOICES THAT MATTER

VISIT OUR WEB SITE

WWW.NEWRIDERS.COM

On our Web site you'll find information about our other books, authors, tables of contents, indexes, and book errata. You will also find information about book registration and how to purchase our books.

EMAIL US

Contact us at this address: **nrfeedback@newriders.com**

- If you have comments or questions about this book
- To report errors that you have found in this book
- If you have a book proposal to submit or are interested in writing for New Riders
- If you would like to have an author kit sent to you
- If you are an expert in a computer topic or technology and are interested in being a technical editor who reviews manuscripts for technical accuracy
- To find a distributor in your area, please contact our international department at this address. **nrmedia@newriders.com**

- For instructors from educational institutions who want to preview New Riders books for classroom use. Email should include your name, title, school, department, address, phone number, office days/hours, text in use, and enrollment, along with your request for desk/examination copies and/or additional information.
- For members of the media who are interested in reviewing copies of New Riders books. Send your name, mailing address, and email address, along with the name of the publication or Web site you work for.

BULK PURCHASES/CORPORATE SALES

The publisher offers discounts on this book when ordered in quantity for bulk purchases and special sales. For sales within the U.S., please contact: Corporate and Government Sales (800) 382-3419 or **corpsales@pearsontechgroup.com**. Outside of the U.S., please contact: International Sales (317) 581-3793 or **international@pearsontechgroup.com**.

WRITE TO US

New Riders Publishing
201 W. 103rd St.
Indianapolis, IN 46290-1097

CALL US

Toll-free (800) 571-5840 + 9 + 7477
If outside U.S. (317) 581-3500. Ask for New Riders.

FAX US

(317) 581-4663

New Riders

WWW.NEWRIDERS.COM